Blacks and Science Volume One

Blacks and Science Volume One

Ancient Egyptian Contributions to Science and Technology

AND

The Mysterious Sciences of the Great Pyramid

BY

Robin Walker

REKLAW EDUCATION LTD
London (U.K.)

First published as two e-books in 2011 and 2012 by Reklaw Education Limited

Copyright © Reklaw Education Limited 2011, 2012, 2013, 2016

All rights reserved. No part of this publication may be reproduced, stored in a retrieval system, or transmitted by any means, without the prior permission in writing from the publisher, nor be otherwise circulated in any form of binding or cover other than that in which it is published and with a similar condition including this condition being imposed on the subsequent purchaser.

ISBN-13: 978-1489578273

ISBN-10: 1489578277

CONTENTS

Opening Remarks   1

PART ONE: ANCIENT EGYPTIAN CONTRIBUTIONS TO SCIENCE AND TECHNOLOGY   3

Preface   5

Introduction   7

1. Mathematics   11
2. Astronomy   15
3. Medicine and Surgery   22
4. Navigation and Cartography   29
5: Architecture   38
6. Others   46

Bibliography   49

PART TWO: THE MYSTERIOUS SCIENCES OF THE GREAT PYRAMID   53

Preface   55

1. Introducing the Great Pyramid   57
2. What was involved in building the Great Pyramid?   62
3. Mathematical, Astronomical, and Other Enigmas   66
4. Straight out of left field   76

Bibliography   80

PART THREE: AFRICAN PROTO SCIENCE AND TECHNOLOGY	83
Preface	85
African Proto Science and Technology	87
Bibliography	96
PART FOUR: EXCERPT FROM AN INTRODUCTION TO THE HISTORY OF SCIENCE, 1917	*99*
Introduction	101
Excerpt: *Science and practical needs--Egypt and Babylonia*	101
PART FIVE: THE AUTHOR	*111*
Biography of Robin Walker	113
Speaking Engagements	114
Index	117

OPENING REMARKS

Information on Black scientists and inventors is becoming more readily available to the general public and this is a welcome development. The British based company BIS Publications, for example, specialises in producing children's books on Black inventors. Mr Keith Holmes has written a useful volume called *Black Inventors: Crafting Over 200 Years of Success*. However, information specifically on the scientific and technological contributions of the Ancient Egyptians is not as readily available as one might think.

Great books and essays have been written on the topic but many authors have pitched their works above the level of the ordinary reader. Other papers are in difficult-to-find journals and collections. Some writers, in an attempt to bring greater prestige to twentieth century European and European American science, dismiss all ancient science as superstition and error. They emphasize what the Ancient Egyptians did not know as opposed to what they did know.

In this book, *Blacks and Science Volume One*, I bring the information together in one place. I write positively about what the Ancient Egyptians achieved and do not waste ink on what they did not achieve. Finally I present the information in as straightforward and accessible a way as possible.

Should you read this book and learn the information:
* You will gain a greater mastery over Black or African History
* Your knowledge will be the envy of your friends and family
* Learning your historical contributions will skyrocket your confidence and esteem
* Your interest in all areas of human culture will dramatically increase
* You will have a vast reserve of information to pass on to your children

This book is largely a synthesis of my previously published Kindle e-books *Ancient Egyptian Contributions to Science and Technology* combined with *The Mysterious Sciences of the Great Pyramid*. I have also added an essay on African proto science and technology. Moreover there is an additional essay on ancient sciences by Professor Walter Libby.

The feedback I received from these e-books was positive, but many people asked me if it was possible to turn these lecture essays into physical books. After all, not everybody possesses a Kindle! My response was to produce this book *Blacks and Science Volume One*. There are two more books in this series *Blacks and Science Volume Two* and *Three*.

The first part of this book is a general introduction to the role played by the Ancient Egyptians in the origin and evolution of Mathematics, Astronomy, Medicine & Surgery, Navigation & Cartography, Architecture, Construction, Metallurgy and other areas that are more controversial.

The second part of the book focuses on one monument--the Great Pyramid of Giza. In this section, I review the discussions and speculations of what the Ancient Egyptians probably knew about *pi, phi,* the Dimensions of the Earth, etcetera.

The third part of the book details some of the archaeological finds that show evidence of proto science and technology in Africa. This data indicates that the Egyptian scientific and technological culture did not come out of nowhere.

In the fourth part of the book, I reproduce a learned essay on the sciences of the Ancient Egyptians, Iraqis and Syrians by Professor Walter Libby. His essay adds information to the discussion not mentioned elsewhere by me.

Finally, in the fifth part of the book, I introduce the lectures that I teach on these topic areas.

Read and enjoy

Robin Walker 2016

PART ONE

ANCIENT EGYPTIAN CONTRIBUTIONS TO SCIENCE AND TECHNOLOGY

PREFACE

While reading through *The Telegraph*, a Conservative British daily broadsheet, I came across a really interesting commentary by Jim Al-Khalili entitled *Science: Islam's forgotten geniuses* (29 January 2008). The writer suggested why we in the West should have more respect for the contributions of non Western scholarship of the Middle Ages. The article cited an example that perhaps should be better known.

> Next year [says Al-Khalili], we will be celebrating the 200th anniversary of Charles Darwin's birth, and the 150th of the publication of his *On The Origin of Species,* which revolutionised our understanding of biology. But what if Darwin was beaten to the punch? Approximately 1,000 years before the British naturalist published his theory of evolution, a scientist working in Baghdad was thinking along similar lines. In the *Book of Animals,* abu Uthman al-Jahith (781-869), an intellectual of East African descent, was the first to speculate on the influence of the environment on species. He wrote: 'Animals engage in a struggle for existence; for resources, to avoid being eaten and to breed. Environmental factors influence organisms to develop new characteristics to ensure survival, thus transforming into new species. Animals that survive to breed can pass on their successful characteristics to offspring.' There is no doubt that it qualifies as a theory of natural selection.

While this is undoubtedly an exciting and thought-provoking piece of information, a question that is sometimes raised but hardly ever addressed is: what else has African minds contributed to scientific and technological thought?

Western scholars are becoming more open to the contributions of Islamic scholars to the development of science and technology including some of the Black ones. Others are starting to embrace the contributions of the Mesopotamians, Indians and Chinese to science and technology. But where is non-Muslim Africa in this discussion? Where is the African Diaspora in this discussion?

African and African Diasporan science history is a subject that has had too little attention paid to it. Some important writers have ventured into the field; Professor Ivan Van Sertima, Professor Charles S. Finch III, Mr Hunter Havelin Adams III, Professor Cheikh Anta Diop, Dr Louis Haber,

Professor Théophile Obenga and Dr Nnamdi Elleh. This work synthesises their findings and presents the data in an easy to digest, bite-size way.

This part of the book is a general introduction to the role played by the Ancient Egyptians in the origin and evolution of Mathematics, Astronomy, Medicine & Surgery, Navigation & Cartography, Architecture, Metallurgy and other areas that are more controversial.

INTRODUCTION

The basic building blocks of physics are a numerical system that can accommodate the three key ideas of distance, mass and time. Distance is a broad concept which encompasses length in one dimension, area in two dimensions and volume in three dimensions.

The basic building block of chemistry is the atom. Derived from the Ancient Greek concept of *atomos,* meaning indivisible, many early thinkers believed that if any particular substance was broken down to its smallest single unit, that unit could not be divided into anything smaller and thus constituted the foundation building block of all substances. Nowadays, scientists know that the atom is not actually the smallest building block. Moreover, atoms can be divided into even smaller particles. This does, however, show how the Ancient Greek idea has evolved into more complex modern ideas of the constituent elements of an atom.

The Ancient Egyptians, however, were responsible for the birth of all of these concepts. They created a sophisticated numerical system. They had rulers that measured length, clocks that measured time and scales that measured weight. Weight is not exactly the same concept as mass, but the ideas are close.

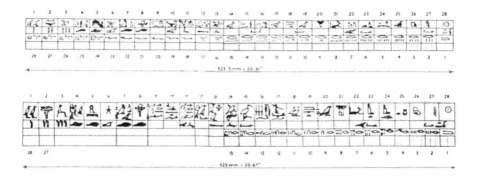

Figure 1. Sketch showing Ancient Egyptian measures of length from the era of Amenhotep I (ruled 1682-1662 BC) of the Eighteenth Dynasty. The primary unit was the royal cubit, the distance from the elbow to the tips of the fingers.

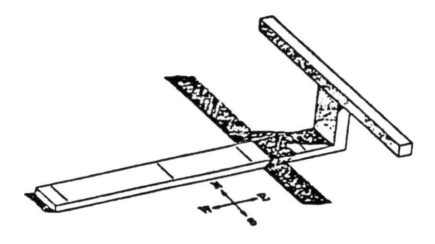

Figure 2. Sketch of an Ancient Egyptian shadow clock from around 1000 BC. Users of the clock typically placed the cross bar facing east in the morning and west in the evening. The hours were read from markings on the horizontal scale.

Figure 3. Taken from the Ancient Egyptian *Book of the Dead* (also called *Coming Forth By Day*), this scene shows the heart of an individual in the Netherworld being weighed against a feather. The idea was that a guilty person would have a heavy heart and an innocent person would have a light heart that would balance the feather. From a scientific perspective, this shows that the Egyptians had clear ideas about measuring weight.

Ancient Egyptian contributions to Science and Technology   9

According to Hunter Adams III, an African American science writer:

> Livio Catullo Stecchini, history of science professor at Harvard University, in an exhaustive study, documents how all contemporary systems of measure are based on standards established by the Egyptians. The Egyptian metrological system coordinated the standard of time--the speed of rotation of one or more points in the vault of heaven with the standard length--the 'cubit' (0.523 meters, originally called the kush), with the standard for weight--the 'qedet' (9 grams) and with the standard for volume--the 'heqat' (4.5 litres). Thus the Egyptian measures of length, weight, volume, as well as time constituted a rational and organic system.

Concerning the concept of the atom, the great scientist Sir Isaac Newton, suggested that the Ancient Greek *atomos* was derived from a concept called the monad, an idea which was ultimately of Ancient Egyptian and Phoenician origin.

Moving from physics and chemistry theories to actual real-world practice, the Egyptians were important inventors and innovators. According to Mr Keith Holmes, an authority on Black inventors, the Ancient Egyptians invented or developed a number of useful products in a variety of industries.

Among these were adhesives (e.g. albumins, beeswax, clay, gelatin, gypsum, natron, starch), made great advances in agriculture (e.g. growing crops of almonds, barley, garlic, ginger, grapes, lentils, palm, sorghum), fermented alcohol (e.g. beer, wine, malts) and made products from animal materials (e.g. bone, butter, cheese, feathers, gut, ivory, mother of pearl, ostrich eggshell, parchment, tortoise shell). They also produced building materials (asphalt, brick, cement, mortar, plaster, sun dried brick), made cosmetics (e.g. perfumes, essential oils, cleansing cream), pioneered certain dyes (e.g. indigo, black, brown, green, red, yellow) and used certain fibres (e.g. cordage, papyrus, also developed techniques in basketry, brushes, matting, weaving). They made glazed ware (e.g. glazed steatite, faience variants, glazed quartz), used gums and resins (e.g. acacia, cedar, copal, frankincense, myrrh, pine), invented various colours of ink (e.g. black, brown, green, blue, white), created a vast range of metals and alloys (e.g. alumina, aluminium, antimony, brass, cobalt, copper, copper-antimony alloy, copper-gold alloy, gold, electrum, hematite, silver, tin) and worked with a variety of minerals (e.g. alum, barites, emery, feldspar, graphite, manganese compounds, mica, sulphur). They used various oils, fats and waxes (e.g. almond oil, belanos oil, bean oil, castor oil, coconut oil, juniper oil, walnut oil), used paints and pigments (e.g. black, blue, grey, orange, pink, red), used various precious and semi-precious stones (e.g. diamonds, emeralds, opal, ruby), and had a well developed industry in pottery (e.g. kilns, moulds, varnishing, polishing). Finally, the Egyptians used spices (e.g. cinnamon, dill, cumin, parsley), created textiles (e.g. cotton, linen) and used a variety of wood in art and building (e.g. Egyptian timber, beech wood, birch, carob-wood, cypresswood, ebony, elm, fig, hornbeams, maple, plywood).

CHAPTER ONE: MATHEMATICS

The Ancient Egyptians made important contributions to the origin and evolution of mathematics. The Ancient Greek scientist, Aristotle, recognised this and wrote the following in his work *Metaphysics:* 'And thus Egypt was the cradle of the mathematical arts.'

Four Ancient Egyptian mathematical documents survive today and have been the subject of considerable research by modern scholars--the *Rhind Papyrus,* the *Berlin Papyrus,* the *Moscow Papyrus* and the *Kahun Papyrus*. These papyri indicate that a large proportion of what we today consider high school mathematics was created by the Ancient Egyptians.

The Egyptians had a decimal system with special symbols for the numbers 1, 10, 100, 1,000, 10,000, 100,000 and 1,000,000. They had fractions, but these were always given as 1/2, 2/3, 1/3, 1/4, 1/5, 1/6, etcetera. With the exception of 2/3, all the other fractions were expressed as one over two, one over three, and so on. These are called unit fractions. If the Ancient Egyptians wanted to express 3/4, they would write 1/2 + 1/4. In a similar vein, if they wanted to express 2/5, they would write 1/3 + 1/15. They were adept at handling fractions. Problem 33 of the *Rhind Mathematical Papyrus,* for example, required the student to calculate 16 + 1/56 + 1/679 + 1/776 + 10 + 2/3 + 1/84 + 1/1358 + 1/4074 + 1/1164 + 8 + 1/112 + 1/1358 + 1/1552 + 2 + 1/4 + 1/28 + 1/392 + 1/4753 + 1/5432 = 37!

The *Rhind Mathematical Papyrus* was probably a Middle Kingdom Period (i.e. Eleventh or Twelfth Dynasty) student's copy book that contains 87 mathematical problems and their solutions. Belonging to an individual student called Ahmose, the text is a record of what he was taught. Beginning with arithmetic and number theory, the student worked with formulae in the areas of algebra, geometry, trigonometry and *pi*. For example, problem 24 asks: 'A quantity plus its seventh becomes 19. What is the quantity?' It required the student to solve for one unknown called 'aha' meaning 'heap'. If problem 24 was written today 'aha' would be transcribed as 'x' and the question would look like this: $x + x/7 = 19$.

Problem 41 asks: 'Find the volume of a cylindrical granary of diameter 9 and height 10.'

Problem 50 addresses the area of circle. The question asks: 'Example of

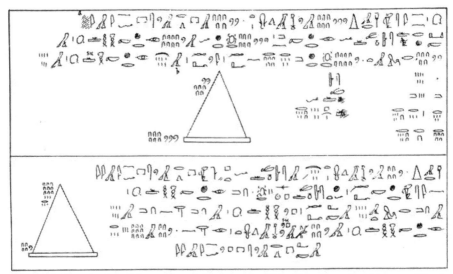

Figure 4. Sketch of problems 56 and 57 from the *Rhind Mathematical Papyrus*. These are the oldest known examples of trigonometry depicted in a mathematical document.

a round field of diameter 9 khet; what is the area?' The suggested formula and method gave an approximation for π as 256/81 which is 3.1605 to 4 decimal places. This is closer to the real figure of π (i.e. 3.14159 etcetera) than the figure 3 used by the Ancient Babylonian mathematicians.

Problem 51 asks: 'A demonstration of the calculation of a triangular plane. If asked: A triangle 10 rods high, 4 at its base; what's its area?'

Problem 52 asks: '[T]rapezium of 20 khet, with a large base of 6 khet and a small base of 4 khet. What is its surface?'

These four problems (41, 50, 51, 52) thus address the volume of a cylinder, the area of a circle, the area of a triangle, and the area of a trapezium. What else is in the papyrus?

Problem 56 asks: 'If a pyramid is 250 cubits high and the side of its base 360 cubits long, what is its seked?' This is a trigonometry problem requiring the student to calculate the seked (or cotangent) of the slope of the pyramid.

Problem 79 asks: 'Inventory of an estate: Houses: 7   Cats: 49   Mice: 343   Barley seeds: 2401   Bushels: 16807.' According to Professor Théophile Obenga, a leading authority on Ancient Egyptian texts, this means: 'Suppose that on an estate of 7 houses, each house had 7 cats, each cat killed 7 mice, each mouse ate 7 barley seeds, and each barley seed would have yielded 7 bushels; how many bushels would that make all told?' In mediaeval times the Italian mathematician Fibonacci wrote: 'Seven old women went to Rome: each woman had seven mules; each mule carried seven sacks: each sack contained seven loaves; and with each loaf were seven knives; each knife was put up in seven sheaths.' This is a seven step geometric progression of 7 x 7 x 7 x 7 x 7 = 16807. If written today, the question would have said: 'Find the sum of 5 terms of the Geometric Progression whose first term is 7 and whose common ratio is 7.'

The *Moscow Mathematical Papyrus* contains 25 mathematical problems of which Problems 10 and 14 are widely regarded as high points in the evolution of Ancient Egyptian mathematics.

Problem 10 asks: 'Method of calculating a basket. If it is said to thee, a basket with an opening of 4 1/2 in its containing, Let me know its surface.' The term basket means 'hemisphere.' Thus, the problem concerns the difficult problem of calculating the surface area of a hemisphere. The formula the scribe used was S = 2d x (8/9) x (8/9) x d, where S is the surface area and d is the diameter, which is almost equivalent to $S = 2\pi r^2$, the way the formula is presented today. The only difference is that the Egyptians reckoned π to be 256/81 or 3.1605.

Problem 14 asks: 'Method of calculating a truncated pyramid. If it is said to thee, a truncated pyramid of 6 ellen in height, of 4 ellen of the base, by 2 of the top.' The solution used the formula of V = h/3 (a^2 + ab + b^2) where V is the volume, a is the base, b is the length of the top, and h is the height. Historians of science and mathematics claim that this method has not been improved on in 4000 years!

The *Berlin Mathematical Papyrus* contains formulae for solving for two unknowns. Problem 1 asks: 'How to divide 100 into two parts such that the square root of one part is 3/4 of the square root of the other part.' In modern algebraic expressions, it looks like this: $x^2 + y^2 = 100$, where y = 3/4x. Other scholars present it like this: $x^2 + y^2 = 100$, where 4y - 3x = 0. Either way, everyone agrees that this problem requires calculating two unknowns, x and y, from two simultaneous equations.

The *Kahun Papyrus* Plate VIII has a mathematical problem on it that has baffled scholars. Professor Cheikh Anta Diop, the brilliant Senegalese scholar, speculates that it is dealing with the volume of a sphere with a hemisphere of 8 units in diameter. Other writers holding a different opinion think it concerns the volume of a cylindrical silo of 8 units in diameter and 12 units it height.

The Ancient Egyptians made other contributions to mathematics that I shall summarise briefly. They pioneered the 3, 4, 5 triangle which is the

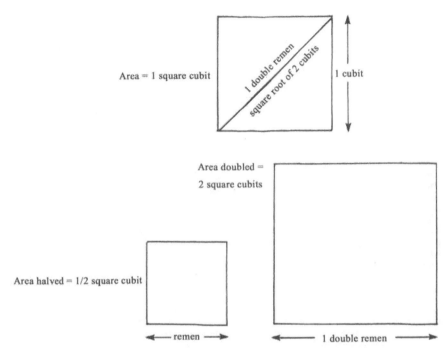

Figure 5. As Professor Beatrice Lumpkin points out with these squares, there is a demonstrable relationship between an Egyptian royal cubit and another Egyptian measurement called a double remen. A double remen is equal to the square root of 2 royal cubits. This is particularly interesting because the square root of 2 equals 1.4142 etcetera. It is an irrational number. Many scholars see this as convincing evidence that the Ancient Egyptians were familiar with the concept of irrational numbers.

basis of the so-called 'Pythagorean Theorem.' They used this triangle to accurately calculate right angles. That the Egyptians knew this triangle, the following excerpt by Plutarch, the great Greco-Roman scholar, is most edifying: 'The Egyptians appeared to have figured out the world in the form of the most beautiful of triangles ... This triangle, the most beautiful of triangles, has its vertical side composed of three, its base of four, and its hypotenuse of five parts, and the square of the latter is equal to the sum of the squares of the two sides.'

Finally, there is evidence of a more controversial and contested nature that the Old Kingdom Egyptians knew about irrational numbers. Many scholars credit the Egyptians with the knowledge of the square root of 2 (1.4142), a more detailed understanding of *pi* or π (3.14), and also *phi* or φ (1.618). This data was built into the proportions of the Great Pyramid of Giza.

CHAPTER TWO: ASTRONOMY

Astronomy is the science of mapping the heavenly bodies including the sun, the moon, the stars and the other planets. Throughout the ages, humans have used astronomy to tell the time, devise calendars, orientate buildings and as a guide to travel.

The Ancient Egyptians pioneered the use of the sundial, the clepsydra (water clock) and the merkhet (i.e. a device using a straight edge and a plumb line to measure stars). The Ancient Egyptians also wrote texts on astronomy that were famous in Greek and Roman times but unfortunately have not survived into our times. One document was called *On the Disposition of Fixed Stars and Stellar Phenomena*. Another text was entitled *On the Disposition of the Sun, Moon and Five planets*. Yet another document was called *On the Syzygies and Phases of the Sun and Moon*. A fourth text was called *On Risings*.

Duncan MacNaughton, author of the erudite *A Scheme of Egyptian Chronology*, reproduced an image of the astronomical ceiling in the Tomb of Senenmut, a contemporary of Hatshepsut (seventeenth century BC). The ceiling has twelve months of the year depicted. He also reproduced a

Figure 6. Water clock from Karnak used for estimating the time over the twelve hours of night.

picture of the heavens from the Ramesseum (fourteenth century BC), again with the twelve months of the year depicted.

The Ancient Egyptians invented the 365 day solar calendar based on astronomical observation. They also created the concept of the month and the zodiac based on the grouping of stars. They grouped at least 43 stellar constellations.

Their most important contribution to astronomy, however, was the creation of the Sothiac or Sothic Cycle which is superior to the leap year that we use today. The Sothiac Cycle is based on the fact that the earth spins 365¼ times each time it orbits the sun. Since it is impractical to have the concept of ¼ of a day, we moderns have adopted the practice of having a leap year of 366 days once every four years to 'correct' for this problem.

The Ancient Egyptians had a cleverer way of dealing with this. They ran a civil calendar of 365 days but also ran a more accurate calendar of 365¼ days at the same time. After one year, the two calendars would disagree by ¼ of a day. After two years, the two calendars would disagree by ½ a day. After three years, the two calendars would disagree by ¾ of a day. After four years, the two calendars would disagree by a whole day. We can

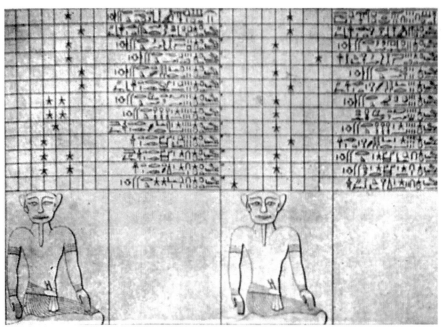

Figure 7. Detail from a star calendar from the time of Rameses VI of the Twentieth Dynasty which, according to Duncan MacNaugton, represents 'a star calendar for each of the twelve hours of night on the 1st and 16th of each month of the year.'

therefore calculate that after eight years, the two calendars would disagree by two days. After twelve years, the two calendars would disagree by three days, etcetera. Keeping these calculations going, after 1460 years of 365¼ days, the two calendars would disagree by a whole year and thus the first day of the year on one calendar would be the first day of the year on the second calendar! The 1460 year period is called the Sothiac Cycle.

A Roman scholar called Censorinus stated that the two Egyptian calendars met up with each other in 139 AD. This meant that the two calendars met up with each other 1460 years earlier i.e. 1321 BC. The two calendars met up with each other 1460 years before this, i.e. 2781 BC. Finally, the two calendars met up 1460 years before this, i.e. 4241 BC. Thus the Egyptian astronomers did not need to use the concept of a leap year.

Concerning the origin of the zodiac, there was a lively battle between Sir E. A. Wallis Budge and Dr Albert Churchward in the early twentieth century over whether the Ancient Egyptians or the Ancient Greeks invented it. The argument centred on the zodiac painted on the ceiling of the Temple of Hathor at Denderah. The temple was known to have been very ancient and may have dated to the time of Fourth Dynasty Pharaoh Khufu (4824-4761 BC). However, the temple standing there today was renovated in the time of the Greek rulers of Egypt, the Ptolemaic Dynasty. So the controversy is this: Did the Greeks add the zodiac to the renovated building or was it there in Pre-Greek times possibly as early as the time of Khufu?

A careful examination of the Denderah Zodiac shows that the image of Cancer is not a crab, as one might expect, but it is actually Khepera the dung beetle. The significance is this. Europe does not have dung beetles, and thus Europeans changed the dung beetle into a crab. Therefore, had the Greeks invented the zodiac they would have placed a crab there instead of a dung beetle. We conclude therefore that Dr Churchward was correct. There was, however, Greek influence on this zodiac. Two of the animals are depicted looking to the side and are shown with dramatic poses that differ from the stiff formalism of Ancient Egyptian art. All the other animals show the stiff formalism of Ancient Egyptian art. It is thus easy to distinguish Egyptian originals from the Greek influences. This all combines to suggest that the Denderah Zodiac was indigenous in origin.

The Roman geographer Strabo wrote a comment in his *Geography* which was most edifying on this subject:

> The Greeks lacked knowledge of the real length of the year and several similar facts until translations of the memoirs of Egyptian priests into the Greek language spread these ideas among astronomers, who have continued to this day to rely heavily on this same source.

Figure 8. Sketch of the Denderah Zodiac from a controversial Egyptian Temple built by the Egyptians but renovated by the Greeks. Who was responsible for the zodiac?

The zodiac divides the year into twelve houses or constellations. This is one of the ways that the concept of the twelve months of the year came about. If the Ancient Greeks lacked indigenous knowledge of the true length of the year they could not have divided it into the twelve months.

The Ancient Egyptians pioneered the heliocentric theory i.e. the idea that the earth and the planets orbit the sun (says Sir Isaac Newton). They knew of the planets Mercury, Venus, Mars, Saturn and Jupiter. The year is, of course, the orbit of Earth around the Sun. The month is, of course, the orbit of the Moon around the Earth. They calculated and predicted lunar eclipses. This is where the earth comes between the sun and the moon, which causes

Ancient Egyptian contributions to Science and Technology

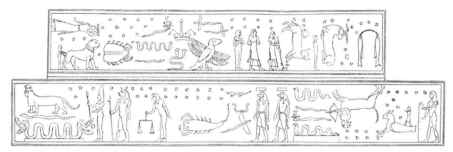

Figure 9. Zodiac from the Temple of Esneh. Duncan MacNaughton feels that this 'may be a late version of an earlier zodiac.' In support of this idea, he points out that: 'The zodiac also has the peculiarity that before the sign Virgo a Sphinx is inserted, a lion with the head of a woman, surely a symbol of the transition from Virgo to Leo. This suggests that the colossal Sphinx carved out of rock near the pyramids of Cheops and Kephren belongs to the same period. It is usually attributed to Kephren and therefore if from internal evidence the date of this zodiac can be fixed we obtain a probable date for Kephren.' If MacNaughton is correct about this, then the original on which it was based would go back to the Fourth Dynasty i.e. to the time of Khehpren better known as Khafra, the son of Khufu mentioned earlier.

the earth to throw its shadow over the moon. Moreover, the Egyptians invented the hour. This is the length of time it takes the moon to move its own diameter relative to the sun.

The earth wobbles as in spins, just like a spinning top. This produces two measurable effects as far as we earthlings are concerned, the precession of the equinoxes and the changes in the circumpolar constellations.

The precession of the equinoxes can be explained as the very slow, cyclic changes in the coordinates of the fixed stars that takes place over a time period of approximately 25,900 years. This enormous period of time is called a Great Year (of 25,900 years) and can be divided into smaller units called an Age or a Great Month (of 2,160 years). Twelve Great Months is equal to one Great Year (i.e. 2160 x 12 = 25,920). The Ancient Egyptians discovered this when they noticed that when the sun rose on the morning of the Spring Equinox, the longest day of the year, there was a particular zodiacal constellation on the Eastern horizon where the sun rose. On each Spring Equinox, they expected to see the same zodiacal constellation. However, after a period of 2160 years, the zodiacal constellation at the Spring Equinox where the sun rose changed to the next zodiacal constellation. After another period of 2160 years, the Spring Equinox would change to the next zodiacal constellation. It would take a Great Year of approximately 25,900 years to complete the cycle to where the sun would rise on the morning of the Spring Equinox where the first zodiacal constellation would be on the Eastern horizon. This phenomenon is called the precession of the equinoxes because the changes to the zodiacal sign over each Great Month goes backwards (i.e. the precession) to the previous zodiacal sign and not forwards to the next zodiacal sign as one would expect.

Other scholars present this information in other ways. According to George Goodman:

> Our entire solar system with all its planets and moon describes a huge circle around another sun in space, viz., the star Sirius. This movement takes 25,920 years to complete and, during that time, our Sun appears [to us earthlings] to traverse through various constellations or star clusters ... By arbitrarily dividing that huge circle into twelve sections (or houses) they gave to each of them an appropriate sign and name and called the duration of 2,160 years an age. Twelve of these ages constitute one complete turn of our solar system around Sirius.

Sir Norman Lockyer, the great English astronomer, proved that the Ancient Egyptians knew this by showing that the Egyptians re orientated their temples to keep them in line with shifting stellar phenomena over the thousands of years.

The circumpolar constellations can be described as the constellations that the North Pole of the earth would point to if it was extended into space. It is considered a pole, because these are the constellations that appear to change their positions THE LEAST as the earth turns on its axis. However, changes in the circumpolar constellations take place every 3,700 years. In the period of a Great Year they change seven times (i.e. $3700 \times 7 = 25,900$).

A number of scholars writing over the last two hundred years believe that the Ancient Egyptians discovered both phenomena; the precession of the equinoxes and the changes in the circumpolar constellations. Some of these writers also claim that the Ancient Egyptians began calculating both phenomena beginning 10,858 BC. As an example, Richard Allen wrote:

> Many have maintained that Egypt was the first to give shapes and names to the star-groups; Dupuis, perhaps inspired by Macrobius of our 5th century, tracing the present solar zodiac to that country and placing its date 13,000 years anterior to our era.

Professor Théophile Obenga, the great Congolese Egyptologist, noticed some interesting scientific ideas hidden in two Egyptian religious hymns. Pharaoh Akhenaten of the Eighteenth Egyptian Dynasty wrote *The Great*

Ancient Egyptian contributions to Science and Technology

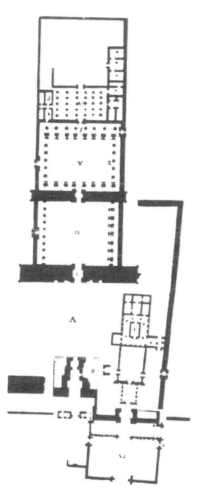

Figure 10. Sir Norman Lockyer suggested that the altered plan of some of the temples, such as this one at Medinet Habu, was a response to the precession of the equinoxes.

Hymn to Aten. A passage in the hymn read as follows: 'Living sun disk, you who brought life into being ... trees and grass grows green ... your rays reach deep into the great green sea.' Professor Obenga noticed the link between sunlight giving life and the colour green. He believes that this is an early understanding of the concepts that we moderns would call photosynthesis and chlorophyll.

Stele 826 in the British Museum contains the text of *Hymn to Amen Ra*. A passage from this hymn read as follows: 'In one short day you voyage millions of leagues and hundreds of thousands. Each day is just an instant for you.' Professor Obenga noticed that this is a reference to the vast speed at which light travels. The actual figure is 5 hours from the Sun to Pluto, the farthest planet.

CHAPTER THREE: MEDICINE AND SURGERY

The Ancient Greek poet, Homer, stated that: 'In medical knowledge, Egypt leaves the rest of the world behind.'

According to the Ancient Egyptian historian Manetho, Pharaoh Djer (5581-5524 BC), of the First Dynasty, wrote a book on anatomy. The same historian reported that Pharaoh Djet (5507-5476 BC), also of the First Dynasty, wrote a famous medical text. Scholars today believe they have identified the Djet era text. They think it has survived as the *Edwin Smith Surgical Papyrus*.

The *Edwin Smith Papyrus* is now housed in the New York Academy of Medicine. It was one of ten surviving Ancient Egyptian medical texts. It describes 48 cases of bone surgery and of external pathology. It demonstrates a detailed knowledge of anatomy, gives remarkably accurate descriptions of traumatic surgical lesions, and describes their treatments where applicable.

Though written during the Eighteenth Egyptian Dynasty, it is a copy of a much older Egyptian text. The Eighteenth Dynasty copyist included glossaries for the readers because the original language nearly 3,000 years earlier was just too archaic.

What has survived is only one third of the original manuscript that stops at the 48th case. Consequently it deals only with the skeletal and soft tissue parts of the head and neck, i.e. the upper portion of the body. It uses nearly 100 anatomical terms in the head and neck regions.

Each case is written out as (i) an examination, (ii) a diagnosis, (iii) a treatment (iv) and finally, glossaries to explain the First Dynasty language to an Eighteenth Dynasty surgeon.

Professor Charles Finch, a medical doctor, who has made a special study of the contents of this papyrus, was somewhat baffled by the standards of medical knowledge achieved. He notes that:

> Cases 29-33 all represent additional case descriptions of vertebral dislocations and sub-luxations and their clinical consequences. At present, some of these conditions are almost impossible to detect or describe fully without X-ray studies. The question then arises is how did our ancient surgeon, living a[n]d

Ancient Egyptian contributions to Science and Technology

Figure 11. Detail from the *Edwin Smith Papyrus.*

practicing [thousands of] years ago, manage to diagnose and describe these problems without benefit of X-rays?

To answer Professor Finch, we just don't know.

Professor Théophile Obenga was also impressed with this document. Case 31 deals with a fracture causing a dislocation of the cervical vertebrae. This led to quadriplegia in the patient. This case demonstrates that the Egyptians understood the connections between injuries to the central nervous system and peripheral damage elsewhere. This implies they recognised the unity of the nervous system and the interconnection of central and peripheral nerves.

Professor Finch informs us that the Ancient Egyptians had a total of perhaps 200 terms for the different parts of the human body that appear in their papyri. There are Ancient Egyptian terms for bones of the head--the

Figure 12. Detail of a wall carving showing a person setting a dislocated shoulder.

cranium, cranial vault, cranial sutures, suture membrane, superciliary arch, orbit, mandibular notch, the internal auditory canal and the external auditory canal. There are terms for the soft tissue parts including the meninges, cerebrum, convolutions of the brain, nasal fossa, nasal cartilage, pharynx, spinal cord, larynx, and oesophagus. For the skeleton, there are terms for the manubrium, sternum, patella, clavicles, scapula, humerus and thoracic vertebra. For the internal organs, there are terms for the liver, intestine, lung, pericardium, stomach, spleen, pancreas, kidney and bladder. Finally there are terms for cerebral spinal fluid, the blood vessel network, the spinal-cord, et cetera.

It should also be borne in mind that with thousands of years of practising mummification, the Ancient Egyptians amassed an array of knives, scalpels and surgical techniques. They used red hot implements to seal off bleeding. They closed wounds with adhesive tape or sutures. Mummification itself took a team of skilled medical personnel perhaps 70 days to complete. Among the many actions needed to complete a mummification, involved evisceration, removing the brain, desiccation, washing the body inside and out using natron, anointing the purified body with aromatic oils and herbs, and wrapping the body in endless bandages. Among the chemical substances involved in the process were palm wine, various spices, perfumes, myrrh, aniseed, onions and natron.

Professor Théophile Obenga was very impressed with the *Ebers Papyrus* and describes it as humanity's first medical encyclopaedia. It has chapters on intestinal disease, ophthalmology, dermatology, gynaecology, obstetrics, pregnancy diagnosis, contraception, dentistry, surgical treatment of abscesses, tumours, fractures and burns. The *Papyrus* has a section on the movement of the heart and pulse cited from and older text called *The Book of the Heart and Vessels*. This document describes how the heart pumps blood around the body. What it did not say was that the blood returns to the heart. It was this discovery that made William Harvey, the seventeenth century English scholar, famous. The *Papyrus* also describes in arcane and picturesque language certain heart ailments such as angina pectoris and Stokes-Adams attacks. Finally, the *Ebers Papyrus* has a section on diagnostic percussion.

Some earlier writers were of the opinion that the Egyptians knew nothing about the function of the brain. Professor Finch points out that Egyptian art shows the raised serpent coming out of the vertex of the cranium on the Pharaonic headdress. He believes that the position of the serpent symbolically divides the cranium into two equal halves or hemispheres. Moreover, the Ancient Egyptian word for the cranial vertex is *wpt* which means to open, to discern, or to judge. The Ancient Egyptian word for cerebrum is *âmm* and means to know and to understand. This shows that the Egyptians knew that the brain was connected to knowing, understanding, judging, and discernment. Professor Obenga points out that Case 22 of the *Edwin Smith Papyrus* shows that brain damage can impair a patient's ability to speak.

In the Old Kingdom Period (i.e. Dynasty One to Six), the doctors were specialists--they focussed on just the eyes, head, teeth, or intestines, etcetera. There was even a separate guild of bone setters who treated fractures and dislocations and pioneered the very same techniques that Hippocrates, the Ancient Greek scholar, would popularise thousands of years later. The Egyptian medical doctors were employed by the state. One Old Kingdom position was 'Chief of Dentists and Physicians.' Another position was 'Director of the Women Doctors.'

Incidentally, nearly 120 physicians appear in the Egyptian annals. Typically, they were trained in an institution called the 'per ankh.' At once, this served as a school, library, clinic, temple and seminary. Much of the teaching and training was taught orally as was done elsewhere in Africa.

Described in both the *Edwin Smith* and the *Ebers Papyri*, the Ancient Egyptian doctors pioneered the use of the diagnostic method. Thus, the patient describes the complaint to the doctor. The doctor then assessed the patient checking over the face, the eyes, nasal secretions, perspiration, and testing for stiffness of limbs or the abdomen. The doctor would ask for a urine and a faeces sample. They took the patients pulse. We know that the Egyptians invented the hour but they must also have invented smaller units of time. Did they invent the minute and the second also? Finally, the doctor percussed the abdomen or chest of the patient.

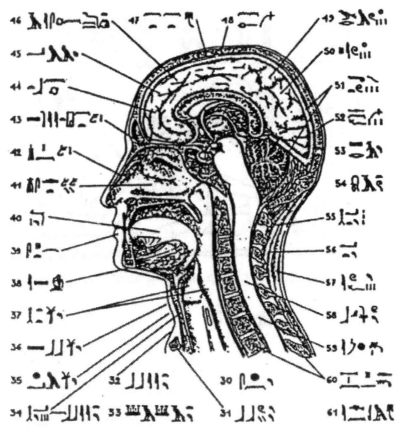

Figure 13. The Ancient Egyptians had anatomical terms for parts of the brain and other anatomical features of the head, many of which have been identified here.

The Ancient Egyptians used a *Materia Medica* of 1,000 animal, plant and mineral products. This is a large pharmacopeia since they could also combine these animal, plant and mineral products. They used moulds from bread, i.e. from the penicillium family, internally and externally to treat infections. Thus they created the first antibiotic. They used poppy extract, i.e. opium, to treat colicky babies and as a sedative and pain killer. They used ox livers, rich in vitamin A, to treat night blindness. They used onions, rich in vitamin C, to treat scurvy. They used Mandrake or related plants for sedation and to treat eye disorders. They used honey combined with grease as a wound salve. This has been shown to speed up the healing of wounds and reduce infections. Finally, they dispensed prescriptions as pills, enemas, suppositories and elixirs.

Ancient Egyptian contributions to Science and Technology

Figure 14. Statuette of Imhotep, the great Third Dynasty era Prime Minister, Architect and Medical Doctor. He has handsome African features typical of the Ancient Egyptians during this period of history.

Imhotep, a Third Dynasty Prime Minister, was the first great individual in recorded history. Before him, history was strictly about Gods and Kings. Imhotep was an intellectual of wide interests including medicine. In western culture, it has become customary to give credit to the Greek scholar Hippocrates as the pioneering medical doctor. Medical practitioners today have the option of swearing on the Hippocratic Oath to promise that they will do no harm to their patients. However, the Oath is dedicated to the gods Apollo and Aesculapius. Aesculapius is none other than Imhotep!

Even more embarrassing, Professor Cheikh Anta Diop reports the following information:

> Theophrastus, Dioscorides, and Galen perpetually cite the prescriptions that they received from the Egyptian physicians, or more specifically, as Galen says, that they had learned by consulting the works conserved in the library of the

Temple of Imhotep at Memphis, which was still accessible in the second century A.D., and where, seven centuries before, Hippocrates, the 'father of medicine' was taught.

The Ancient Egyptians also invented a contraceptive solution. It was a concoction whose active ingredient was a spermicide that did actually kill sperm.

They also pioneered a pregnancy test which involved sprinkling urine of a possibly pregnant woman on barley to test how the barley grew. Modern scholars say this test was 40% successful. This is a low figure, but we must remember that modern pregnancy tests are far from reliable!

Finally, the Kushites in the land to the south of Egypt also made use of antibiotics. They pioneered in the use of tetracycline.

CHAPTER FOUR: NAVIGATION AND CARTOGRAPHY

It may surprise readers to know that Africa has contributed a lot more to shipping, navigation and map making than many of us have been led to suspect. Maritime activity has a long history in Africa. In the time of Pharaoh Sneferu (4872-4824 BC) of the Fourth Egyptian Dynasty, the *Palermo Stone Annals* record that 40 ships returned from Canaan in the Middle East laden with cedar trunks. An Egyptian ship from the time of Khufu, his son, has survived and has been reassembled. Professor Finch says that it was '25 feet longer than Columbus' flagship, the *Santa Maria*.'

The Greek historian Diodorus Siculus reported that the largest ship in the fleet of 'Sesostris' was 480 feet long. However, when the Greeks speak of Sesostris, sometimes they mean the Twelfth Dynasty rulers Senwosret I, II, or III. Other times they mean Rameses II of the Nineteenth Dynasty. We therefore cannot be sure of whom Diodorus was speaking. Which ever be the case, one of the Twelfth or Nineteenth Dynasty ships was four times the length of Columbus' *Santa Maria*.

Pharaoh Hatshepsut (1650-1600 BC) of the Eighteenth Dynasty commanded a voyage to Punt. Scholars are unsure of where this country was but the general view is that it was either Ethiopia or Somalia. The wall frescoes in Hatshepsut's Temple in Deir-el-Bahri depict the main vessel with its sails. Even more impressive, however, were the obelisk barges used in Hatshepsut's time to move the vast obelisks from Aswan to Karnak. Professor John Pappademos, a modern authority on Ancient Egyptian science and technology, wrote:

> The obelisk barges of Queen Hatshepsut have been estimated at 95 metres in length, with a beam of 32 metres and a deadweight of 2500 tons. Such a barge would dwarf Lord Nelson's flagship the H.M.S. Victory at the battle of Trafalgar.

Since the Ancient Egyptians had sophisticated shipping, a question has been raised about whether or not they visited Ancient America. A generation ago, Norwegian explorer, Thor Heyerdahl, set about testing this theory. He wanted to know whether Africans had visited the Americas

30   Ancient Egyptian contributions to Science and Technology

Figure 15. Constructed in traditional style, this is Ra I photographed on the high seas in 1969.

before 1492, the time of Columbus. He hired expertise from the Baduma People of Lake Chad led by Mr Abdullah Djibrine, and commissioned them to build a boat in traditional style from papyrus reeds. They built and launched the ship, sailing from Safi in North Africa across the Atlantic, but there was one key fixture missing from the ship.

Unfortunately, the ship, Ra I, disintegrated. The missing fixture held the key to why the voyage failed. However, the failed ship STILL GOT

Ancient Egyptian contributions to Science and Technology

ALMOST AS FAR AS BARBADOS! Thus, it was indeed possible that early Africans had the technology to visit the Americas well before 1492. Thor Heyerdahl wrote a 1971 book on his experience *The Ra Expedition,* and a 1972 television documentary.

There were a number of great Native American Civilisations that existed in Ancient and Mediaeval times. Among these were the Olmecs, but also the civilisations of the Mayans, the Incas, the Mixtecs and the Aztecs.

The first or oldest was the Olmec Civilisation (*c.*1200-400 BC). Olmec apparently means 'People of the Jaguar.' The other Native American civilisations developed from the Olmec base and thus the Olmec Civilisation is the most important and ultimately the most controversial.

In 1858 the first major relic of Olmec art was found by peasants at a Mexican village called Tres Zapotes. It was a colossal stone head, 8 feet high and weighed 10 tons. In 1862 José M. Melgar found a second stone

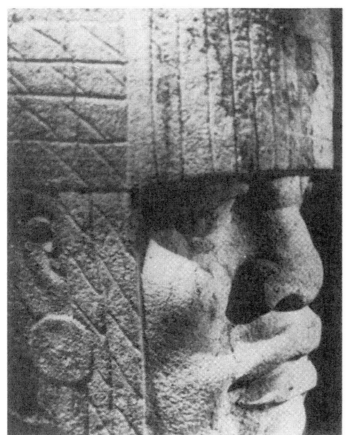

Figure 16. Superb colossal stone head found at San Lorenzo showing African facial features and well over two thousand years old.

head. Unlike the earlier peasants, Melgar was in a position to write up and draw scholarly attention to his findings. His report appeared in the *Mexican Society of Geography and Statistics* in 1869. A key statement in the report read as follows: 'I reflected that there had undoubtedly been Negroes in this country, and that this had been in the first epoch of the world.'

In 1939 the Smithsonian Institute and National Geographic commissioned Mr and Mrs Matthew Stirling to remove the heads. Since then, a further fourteen Olmec stone heads have been found. Two from Tres Zapotes, four from La Venta, six from San Lorenzo and the remaining four from a number of other sites.

How do we interpret this data?

A number of scholars have presented ideas that could well shed light on this issue. Professor Ivan Van Sertima wrote *They Came Before Columbus* in 1977. Dr Andrej Wiercinski presented a paper which appeared in the *Proceedings of the 41st International Congress of the Americanists* in 1974. Count Alexander Von Wuthenau wrote *Art of the World: Pre-Columbian Terracottas* in 1969. Rafique Ali Jairazbhoy wrote *Ancient Egyptians and Chinese in America* in 1974. Finally, Professor Charles Hapgood wrote *Maps of the Ancient Sea Kings* in 1966. He does not address the Olmec issue directly, concentrating instead on the Piri Re'is Map of 1512/1513, but his findings do impact on our understanding of this tantalising issue.

Professor Ivan Van Sertima was a Guyanese anthropologist turned historian. In *They Came Before Columbus*, 1977, he identifies the helmets worn by the Olmec heads as the military helmets worn by Nubian soldiers during the late Egyptian periods. However, he denies that the Olmecs were Africans. He is clear that the Olmecs were Native Americans. He does, however, infer that Africans were highly esteemed among their Native American hosts. Hence the Olmecs making the massive stone heads depicting the Africans and erecting pyramids in the African style.

Van Sertima also highlights cultural similarities of a type that one might expect if one culture influences another. For example, the pharaohs of Africa's Nile Valley wore a red and white double crown. There is an image of an Olmec dignitary at Cerro de la Piedre wearing a double crown. Secondly, the pharaohs wore a false beard that supposedly represented age and wisdom. In Native American art there are false beards depicted on distinguished persons. Thirdly, the flail is a symbol of authority held by African kings and chief dignitaries. There is a painting at Oxtotitlan of a man holding a flail in an African manner. Fourthly, purple was a symbol of royalty and for priests in the Nile Valley yet there is a San Lorenzo head painted purple.

Professor Beatrice Lumpkin is a mathematician who became part of the Van Sertima Journal of African Civilisations team. She wrote a paper called *Pyramids--American and African: A Comparison* where she points out that both the Mexican and African Pyramids have a north-south orientation and both functioned as astronomical observatories.

Dr Andrej Wiercinski, a Polish craniometrist, presented a paper published in the *Proceedings of the 41st International Congress of the Americanists* in 1974 based on research he completed in 1972. He examined skeletal remains from 2 elite Olmec burial sites and found that at Tlatilco, the earlier site, 13.5% of the individuals buried there were Africans. At the later site of Cerro de las Mesas, 4.5% of the individuals buried there were Africans. The burials had African males interred next to Native American females.

How should this be interpreted?

This may well indicate that the African visitors to Mexico joined the elites. It may also suggest husband and wife burials. The data may well be evidence that the Africans were being absorbed by the Native Americans through intermarriage. This may explain how 13.5% eventually became 4.5%.

There are, however, SEVERE weaknesses with Wiercinski's methodology and thus his findings need a careful interpretation. The weaknesses, however, are not what his many critics claim it is. His criteria for determining who belonged to what race was not overly lax when it came to identifying Africans but on the contrary, he was overly strict. Thus many African skulls that are genuinely Negro, Wiercinski would have classified as Mulatto. Only those Africans with the most pronounced Negro features would meet Wiercinski's Negro category! Therefore the truer figure for the numbers of Africans in the Olmec burials could have been higher than the figures Wiccinski reported.

Count Alexander Von Wuthenau was a German art historian with a specialism in the art of Ancient Mexico. He was a speaker at an event hosted by President Senghor in Dakar in 1966. He is also the author of *Art of the World: Pre-Columbian Terracottas,* 1969 and *Unexpected faces in Ancient Mexico,* 1976. Count Von Wuthenau also contributed to some of Van Sertima's books. His photographs of Olmec period art are replete with sculptures that clearly depict Africans.

Jacqueline Patten-Van Sertima was the Photographic and Artistic

34   Ancient Egyptian contributions to Science and Technology

Figure 17. In these photographs, Jairazbhoy points out the similarity between the Ancient Egyptian Goddess Nut holding up the sky with the hieroglyphic sign for 'sky' above her head with these ancient Mexicans also holding up the sky. Notice the similar symbols above their heads that closely resemble the Egyptian sign for sky.

Figure 18. In these examples, Jairazbhoy points out the similarity between the two Egyptian deities pouring libation over the head of the pharaoh where the two streams of water cross each other with a scene from an early Mexican codex where two deities pour libations over the head of an individual again with the two streams of water crossing each other.

Ancient Egyptian contributions to Science and Technology 35

Director of the Journal of African Civilizations. She also has photographs of Olmec era art where Africans are clearly depicted.

Rafique Ali Jairazbhoy was an Indian scholar who used to live in Britain. He is an advocate of an idea, once popular among anthropologists called 'diffusionism.' This is the idea that many different cultures had elements that could be traced back to a parent civilisation. This eminently sensible idea fell out of favour when scholars realised that Africa was the cradle of humanity and civilisation. All of a sudden diffusionism became a dirty word not to be used in polite anthropological company. This is still the case today. Whichever be the case, Jairazbhoy wrote *Ancient Egyptians and Chinese in America* in 1974.

Mr Jairazbhoy names the pharaoh who sent the voyages to Ancient America as Rameses III of the Twentieth Dynasty (1230-1199 BC). Citing Egyptian documents that mention that Rameses III sent ships to the ends of the earth and to the mountain in the far west of the world, he identifies these places as Central America. Jairazbhoy shows a huge number of parallels between Olmec Mexico and Nile Valley Africa. In a later book, Jairazbhoy strengthens his claims. He now believes that the Ancient Africans created the Olmec civilisation. The 1992 book is entitled *Rameses III: Father of Ancient America.*

Professor Charles Hapgood, a cartographer then at the University of New Hampshire, wrote *Maps of the Ancient Sea Kings* in 1966. Much of the book deals with the research that him and his doctorate students completed on the Piri Re'is Map of 1512/1513. Piri Re'is was a Turkish admiral of the sixteenth century. He wrote the *Book of Piri Re'is* with the sole aim of discrediting Columbus. Unimpressed by the claim that Columbus had discovered the Americas, Piri Re'is accused Columbus of possessing maps that date back to the time of Alexander the Great that had the Americas already mapped on them. To bolster this claim, Piri Re'is produced his own map which clearly has Brazil and Mexico depicted on it and with a high degree of accuracy. In compiling his own map, Piri Re'is used 30 source maps including at least one from the Egyptian city of Alexandria.

Professor Hapgood and his students, believing that the Alexandrian map or maps were the key to the Piri Re'is map, tried to find the geodetic centre of the original Alexandrian map or maps on which Piri Re'is was based. They found that the geodetic centre was 100 miles west of Syene i.e. Aswan. Thus the original cartographer or cartographers responsible for the key map or maps on which the Piri Re'is Map was based were standing on the ancient border between Nubia and Egypt, 100 miles west of Aswan!

Ancient Egyptian contributions to Science and Technology

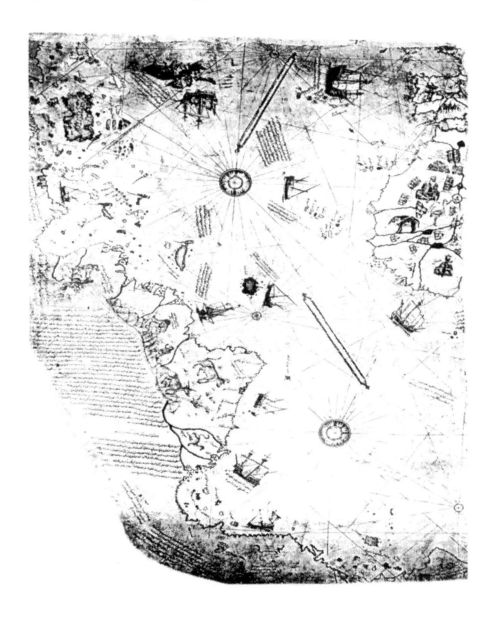

Figure 19. The Piri Re'is Map of 1512 or 1513. It clearly has Brazil and Mexico accurately depicted on it.

So what conclusions should we draw?

Professor Finch cited earlier sees this as proof that Nile Valley Africans from Egypt and Nubia visited the Americas in ancient times and mapped it.

Professor Hapgood and his students point out that the Piri Re'is Map also accurately details Antarctica BEFORE it iced over. They therefore conclude that the key source maps used by Piri Re'is were not just ancient, but were actually pre-historic. While they are sure in locating the geodetic centre of the map 100 miles of Aswan they draw no simple conclusions from this fact. Instead, they conclude on page 194 of their book:

> We shall now assume that some 20,000 or more years ago, while paleolithic peoples held out in Europe, more advanced cultures existed elsewhere on earth, and that we have inherited part of what they once possessed.

We conclude that there were actual contacts between the Nile Valley and Ancient Mexico evidenced by the numerous examples of art and portraiture made by the Native Americans that clearly depict Africans. Agreeing with Van Sertima, we believe that the Olmec Civilisation was an indigenous Native American culture. We further believe that Africans visited them and introduced some new ideas and concepts that influenced Native American art and ritual. Heyerdahl has shown that Africans had the capability to make the voyages and the numerous parallels demonstrated by Van Sertima and Jairazbhoy makes this conclusion inescapable. We believe that the evidence presented by Wiercinsky suggests that Africans intermarried into the Olmec elites and were gradually absorbed. Agreeing with Jairazbhoy, we believe that the voyages from Africa to the Americas took place during the time of Rameses III, if not earlier. Finally, we believe that Professor Finch is correct to infer that early African visitors to the Americas mapped at least some of the Americas and portions of this information has survived in the Piri Re'is Map.

CHAPTER FIVE: ARCHITECTURE

Architecture is a combination of art and technology and often encompasses the uses of many other sciences in construction. A typical building is analysed by its plan, its walling which includes the building materials, the openings (i.e. the doorways and windows), the supports, the roofing, and the ornamentation.

Pharaoh Djoser, the second king of the Third Egyptian Dynasty, ruled between 5018 and 4989 BC. He built the earliest monument in the world still celebrated today. Every year, thousands of tourists visit his Funerary Complex in the city of Saqqara. Imhotep, his celebrated Prime Minister, designed the Complex.

An outer wall, now mostly in ruins, surrounded the whole structure. It was built on a rectangular plan, one mile long, and with one entrance. Through the entrance are a series of columns, the first stone-built columns known to historians. Connected to walls, they are ornamental having been modelled on plant stems grouped together. The North House also has ornamental columns built into the walls that have papyrus-like capitals.

Figure 20. Model reconstruction of the Funerary Complex of Saqqara (c.5000 BC). Built by Pharaoh Djoser, this complex is the oldest surviving great masterwork of architecture in the world.

Ancient Egyptian contributions to Science and Technology 39

Figure 21. Detail from the North House of the Funerary Complex. This monument contains the first attempt to build columns in human history.

Also inside the complex is the Ceremonial Court. Like everything else these buildings are solid and are thus symbolic. The Court is made of limestone blocks that have been quarried and then shaped. In the centre of the complex is the Step Pyramid, the first of 90 Egyptian pyramids. Made of limestone blocks, it is 197 feet high. Unlike the later pyramids, this structure is built on a rectangular plan measuring 345 by 414 feet-- equivalent to a base of 14,000 square yards. It has 6 steps and may represent a stairway. The building slopes at an angle of 72° 30'. Under the Pyramid were a series of rock-hewn chambers and corridors. They are ornamented with panels of colourful tiles. In these hidden quarters, Djoser and eleven others are said to have been buried. On the importance of the Djoser Complex, Professor Finch noted that:

> [It] was humanity's first great architectural triumph. It established architectural forms, styles, and canons still in use today. The practical building technique and masonry evident in the entrance temple were never surpassed, though ... they were realized on a grander scale.

The monuments 'on a grander scale' include the structures built by the Fourth Dynasty Pharaohs--the Step Pyramid of Meidum, the Bent and Red Pyramids of Dashur, and the three Great Pyramids of Giza--monuments built between 4872 and 4615 BC. Of these, the most impressive is the first Great Pyramid of Giza. It was 481 feet tall, the equivalent of a 40 storey building. It was made of 2.3 million blocks of limestone and granite, some weighing 100 tons. The accuracy of the construction work remains astonishing. Dr Alfred Russell Wallace, a famous British scientist, commented on this more than a hundred years ago in an address before the British Association for the Advancement of Science:

> 1. That the pyramid is truly square, the sides being equal, and the angles right angles; 2. That the four sockets on which the first four stones of the corners rested are truly on the same level; 3. That the directions of the sides are accurate to the four cardinal points [of north, south, east and west]; 4. That the vertical height of the pyramid bears the same proportion to its circumference at the base as the radius of a circle does to its circumference [i.e. the Egyptians understood π].

In Part Two of this book, we will have much more to say about this monument.

Pharaoh Senwosret II (3331-3299 BC) of the Middle Kingdom constructed Kahun, a town of officials, priests and workers. It had over a

Ancient Egyptian contributions to Science and Technology

Figure 22. Plan of a part of Kahun, showing houses of similar layouts and streets laid out on a horizontal vertical grid.

hundred houses where even the smallest homes for people of the lowest rank had 4 to 6 rooms and an area of 1,022 square feet or larger.

Excavations revealed that this city was the world's first known example of town planning. Kahun was rectangular and walled. Inside, the city was divided into two parts. One part housed the wealthier inhabitants--the scribes, officials and foremen. The other part housed the ordinary people. The streets of the western section in particular, were straight, laid out on a grid, and crossed each other at right angles. A stone gutter, over half a metre wide, ran down the centre of every street. Positioned to benefit from the cool north winds, five single storey mansions were found along the northern edge of the city. Their doorways were arched. Each boasted 70 rooms, divided into four sections or quarters. There was a master's quarter, quarters for women and servants, quarters for offices and finally, quarters for granaries, each facing a central courtyard. The master's quarters had an open court with a stone water tank for bathing. Surrounding this was a colonnade. Of the maze of rooms, some were barrel vaulted in brick but others were wooden and thatched. The ceilings were supported by wooden and stone columns some with palmiform capitals. Limewash coated the walls, but some rooms contained frescoes.

Amenemhet III (3242-3195 BC) of the same dynasty built at Hawara the Labyrinth with its massive layout, multiple courtyards, chambers and halls. The very largest building in antiquity, it boasted 3,000 rooms. One thousand five hundred were above ground and the other one thousand five hundred were underground. Herodotus, the Ancient Greek historian, saw it in ruins three thousand years later. He was still somewhat impressed:

> I visited this place, and found it to surpass description; for if all the walls and other great works of the Greeks could be put together in one, they would not equal, either for labour or expense, this Labyrinth; and yet the [Greek] temple of Ephesus is a building worthy of note, and so is the temple of Samos. The pyramids likewise surpass description, and are equal to a number of the greatest works of the Greeks; but the Labyrinth surpasses the pyramids.

Further south lay the complex of temples in the city of Waset. The Karnak and Luxor temples, now in partial ruin, were built over many years with contributions from different pharaohs of the Twelfth, Eighteenth, Nineteenth and Twenty-Fifth Dynasties (3405-664 BC). The Karnak Complex was a place of culture and business. It should be thought of as an abbey since people lived and worked there and the complex was self-contained. The treasures of the ancient world passed through its corridors; gold and precious woods from Kush, tribute from Syria, and vases from Crete.

A procession of sphinxes led to the outer pylon, itself 370 feet across, 143 feet high, and 49 feet thick at the base, but becoming narrower at the top. Behind the pylon was the Temple of Amen, which originally had huge doors to close it off. A place of unbelievable luxury, the Hypostyle Hall, just one of its many temples, was 171 feet long and 338 feet wide, covering an area of 56,000 square feet. It was the largest enclosed space in Egyptian architecture, even larger than Durham Cathedral by 5,000 square feet. It contained 134 sandstone columns, covered with bas-reliefs and hieroglyphics. An architect described the Hall as follows:

Ancient Egyptian contributions to Science and Technology 43

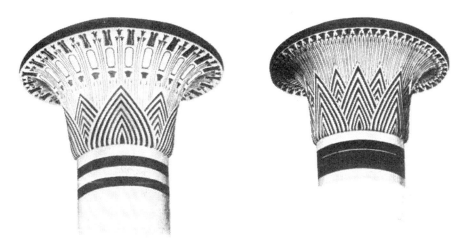

Figure 23. Masterly decorated capitals from columns in the Karnak Complex.

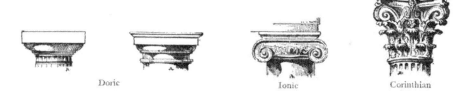

Figure 24. It is not difficult to trace the development of architecture from the Saqqara Complex, through the Karnak Complex to the evolution of Greek architecture. Greek capitals are typically classified as Doric, Ionic or Corinthian.

> No language [says Fergusson] can convey an idea of its beauty, and no artist has yet been able to reproduce its form so as to convey to those who have not seen it any ideas of its grandeur. The mass of its central piers, illuminated by a flood of light from the clerestory, and the smaller pillars of the wings gradually fading into obscurity, are so arranged and lighted as to convey an idea of infinite space; at the same time the beauty and massiveness of the forms, and the brilliancy of their coloured decorations, all combine to stamp this as the greatest of man's architectural works.

There were huge obelisks that stood before the façades of the Karnak and Luxor temples. They were made of a single piece of stone that was hewn from a quarry and then transported to the required position. Pharaoh Hatshepsut erected one such obelisk. It was 90.2 feet tall and weighed an astonishing 302 tons. There is a huge and unfinished obelisk that is 41.78

44 Ancient Egyptian contributions to Science and Technology

Figure 25. While Egyptian temple architecture was magnificent, their domestic architecture was also impressive. This is a reconstruction of an Egyptian Country House.

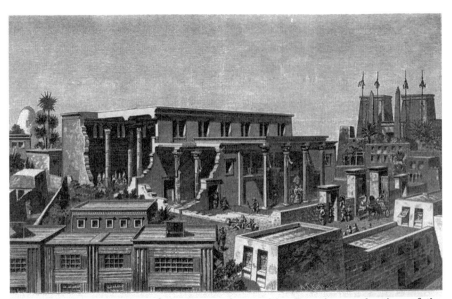

Figure 26. Reconstruction of the house of a wealthy Egyptian at the time of the Eighteenth Dynasty Period.

Ancient Egyptian contributions to Science and Technology

metres long that was left at Aswan, presumably because it did not meet exacting standards of accuracy. The importance of these monuments are such that one authority has argued that there is a typological and symbolic link between the obelisks of ancient times and the skyscrapers of today. As Dr Nnamdi Elleh, an expert in African architecture, put it: 'Several texts exist of Pharaohs boasting that they erected obelisks which reached, pierced, or mingled with the sky.'

Pharaoh Hatshepsut (1650-1600 BC) of the Eighteenth Dynasty was also the builder of one of Egypt's most popular monuments. Senenmut, the Overseer of Works, constructed her temple in the region now known as Deir-el-Bahri.

Rather than build upwards from a base, the Mortuary Temple was built downwards, being cut out of a mountain. The whole building was hewn from the rocks by hammer and chisel. The result is a pillared terrace structure that rises in three stages with 2 central ramps, also carved and sculpted. The ramps are long and slope with a gentle gradient. Their position divides the temple into two symmetrical halves. Entrance halls of limestone columns lead to the interior chapels dedicated to the deities Anubis, Hathor, Osiris and Ra. Through the colonnade, the interior has wall reliefs that depict Hatshepsut's maritime voyages to Punt (i.e. possibly Somalia or Ethiopia) showing also the round houses of that country. In its time, great sculptures embellished the building. There were over 100 limestone sphinxes, 22 granite sphinxes, 40 limestone statues of Hatshepsut, and 28 granite statues of Hatshepsut.

Rameses II (1394-1328 BC) of the Nineteenth Dynasty also built a temple carved out of a hill. The Temple of Abu Simbel, in Nubia, is of an incredible scale.

The façade is 108 feet wide and contains four colossal statues of the pharaoh, each 66 feet high. What is remarkable here is the organisational feat involved. The carved images of Rameses are so large that each builder/sculptor would be so close to their work that none of them would be able to see the bigger picture as they worked. For this reason, accuracy was critical and not just for artistic reasons. The building was oriented to the east to catch the first rays of sunlight that illuminated its icons at the end of a 208 feet corridor. Inside the entrance to the temple are statues of the deity Osiris. This led to a smaller hall that led to an inner chamber.

CHAPTER SIX: OTHERS

Hunter Adams III, an African American science writer, mentions other areas of intellectual activity where the Ancient Egyptians made important contributions--Harmonics, Electroplating and Aeronautics. According to him:

> The Egyptians were the first to formalize the mathematical properties of music ... This mathematical relationship, which results from the phenomenon of classical gravitation, constitutes the essential basis of musical harmony, one of the direct applications of which is the length of a harp string. The longest string emits a sound of a certain pitch. Another string, half this one's length, emits a sound consisting of vibrations twice as rapid, and one octave higher. Thus all the intervals which define the seven notes of the diatonic scale represent the relationship between the string-lengths for any two notes which is the inverse of the relationship between their rates of vibration.

The Ancient Egyptians invented the diatonic scale. This scale is the basis of contemporary western music and its origins can be traced back to flutes that have been discovered in Ancient Egyptian tombs. Thirty of these instruments have been found that play the diatonic scale and Professor Obenga is of the opinion that these flutes have been in use since at least the Fifth Dynasty period.

Adams mentions sophisticated Egyptian metallurgical objects that could only have been produced using very modern techniques:

> Electroplated gold and silver objects have been found in Egypt from roughly the Middle Kingdom ... to the Greek era of the Ptolemies ... Nineteenth-century French archaeologist Auguste Mariette in the *Grand Dictionaire Universal du 10th Siecle* describes such artefacts he found excavating an area near the Sphinx. Wooden flagstaffs about 30 metres tall, placed in front of Egyptian temples from the Middle Kingdom onward, had the top end capped with a sheath of gold-plated copper.

Mr Adams was clearly baffled by this discovery. He asks: 'where did the source of electrical energy to plate one metal onto another come from?

As elsewhere dealing with Ancient Egyptian science and technology, the modern scholar stands somewhat baffled and in awe.

Ancient Egyptian contributions to Science and Technology

Another baffling fact is that perhaps fifteen objects have been discovered in Ancient Egyptian tombs that could be classified as model gliders. Hunter Adams reports on the most famous and controversial example of such a discovery:

> One of the more extraordinary artifacts of ancient Egypt was the discovery in 1898, in a tomb near Saqqara, of a model glider or sailplane made of sycamore wood dating from about [the] third or fourth century B.C. It lay undisturbed, buried in a box of 'bird objects' in room 22 of the Cairo Museum's basement until 1969, when museum archaeologist, Dr Khalil Messiha and his flight engineer brother, Guirguis, rediscovered it. A special research committee was established by the Egyptian Under Secretary of the Ministry of Culture, M. G. Mokhtar, in December of 1971 to investigate it. From their examination of it and bird models in the museum the committee concluded that this object definitely was not a bird - but a model glider.'

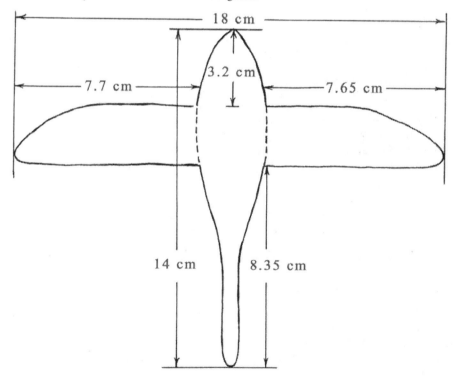

Figure 27. Controversial artefact discovered in 1898 and analysed in 1971. Dr Gamal Mokhtar issued an *Official Statement on the Messiha Discovery* where he stated: 'Few days ago, members of the International Aerospace Education Committee, who met in Cairo for the first time, were surprised when they visited the Egyptian Museum. This was not the normal surprise of visitors coming to the Museum for the first time, but also a surprise to see the model of an aeroplane 2300 years old.'

For some reason, this particular discovery has been cited frequently to discredit African American scholars who have made investigations into the history and culture of Ancient Egypt. There has been a media campaign initiated by various European American scholars to suggest that anyone who says this particular object is a glider and not a bird is a Black scholar making up history. The truth of the situation however, is that no Black scholar was involved in the discovery of the artefact, nor was any Black scholar involved in classifying it as a glider. All of this research work was carried out by contemporary Arab Egyptians.

Professor Finch informs us that the Egyptians were working copper in prehistoric times suggesting dates such as 7500 to 6500 BC. Archaeologists have found copper beads, pins, bracelets, chisels, rings, harpoon heads, needles and tweezers. By the Fourth Dynasty period, bronze artefacts (i.e. copper combined with 4 to 15% tin) have been recovered. The Egyptians were working gold in pre-dynastic times. Archaeologists found gold beads, a golden ring, a gold cylinder seal, vases covered in golden foil, and knives covered in golden foil. Some objects were of gold alloyed to copper or silver. The Egyptians worked iron as early as pre-dynastic times. However, the oldest known significant piece of iron is a portion of a tool found lodged between joints of the masonry of the Great Pyramid of Giza. Finally, the Egyptians were working steel (i.e. iron combined with carbon) by 1200 BC. Two knife blades were found made of low carbon steel of 0.7%.

Mr Adams brilliantly summed up the important role of Ancient Egypt in the history of science and technology and we give him the final word:

> To them, we owe the concepts of most of the fundamental physical quantities: area, volume, weight, distance, density, and time, along with standard units and accurate methods of measurements using these quantities. Regarding technology for example, today's small metal locks and keys owe their basic design to large wooden locks and keys invented 4,000 years ago in Egypt as well as folding beds and chairs. In regard to medicine, they produced the first physicians, the first extensive medical literature and knowledge; the Western medical tradition is an extension of the Egyptian one, and not the Greek. In fact, the Greeks called Egypt the seat of scientific knowledge and sent many of its most brilliant scholars there to study such as Thales, Democritus, and Pythagoras.

BIBLIOGRAPHY

Introduction

Hunter Havelin Adams III, *African & African-American Contributions to Science and Technology,* US, Portland Baseline Essay, 1986, p.21 and Figure 7d

Keith C. Holmes, *Black Inventors. Crafting Over 200 Years of Success,* US, Global Black Inventor Research Projects, 2008, pp.18-19

John Pappademos, *An Outline of Africa's Role in the History of Physics,* from *Blacks in Science: Ancient and Modern,* edited by Ivan Van Sertima, US, Transaction Publishers, 1983, pp.177-196

John Pappademos, *The Newtonian Synthesis in Physical Science and its roots in the Nile Valley,* from *Egypt: Child of Africa,* edited by Ivan Van Sertima, US, Transaction Publishers, 1994, pp.305-322.

Chapter 1: Mathematics

Cheikh Anta Diop, *Civilization or Barbarism,* US, Lawrence Hill Books, 1991, pp.231-278

Charles S. Finch, *The Star of Deep Beginnings,* US, Khenti, 1998, pp.57-91

Beatrice Lumpkin, *Mathematics and Engineering in the Nile Valley,* from *Egypt: Child of Africa,* edited by Ivan Van Sertima, US, Transaction Publishers, 1994, pp.323-340

Théophile Obenga, *African Philosophy: The Pharaonic Period: 2780-330 BC,* Senegal, Per Ankh, 2004, pp.421-498

Claudia Zaslavsky, *The Yoruba Number System,* from *Blacks in Science: Ancient and Modern,* edited by Ivan Van Sertima, US, Transaction Publishers, 1983, pp.113-116

Chapter 2: Astronomy

Cheikh Anta Diop, *Civilization or Barbarism*, US, Lawrence Hill Books, 1991, pp.278-282

Charles S. Finch, *The Star of Deep Beginnings*, US, Khenti, 1998, pp.167-195

George R. Goodman, *The Age of Unreason* from *The Freethinker, Volume 85*, London, 1965, p.182

Duncan MacNaughton, *A Scheme of Egyptian Chronology*, UK, Luzac & Co., 1932, pp.110, 236 and plates III, VII, VIII, X, XI, XII and XIII

Théophile Obenga, *African Philosophy: The Pharaonic Period: 2780-330 BC*, Senegal, Per Ankh, 2004, pp.91-118, 134-146 and 343-344

John Pappademos, *The Newtonian Synthesis in Physical Science and its roots in the Nile Valley*, from *Egypt: Child of Africa*, edited by Ivan Van Sertima, US, Transaction Publishers, 1994, pp.305-322

Chapter 3: Medicine

Hunter Havelin Adams III, *African & African-American Contributions to Science and Technology*, US, Portland Baseline Essay, 1986, pp.45-48 and Figures 25 and 26

Cheikh Anta Diop, *Civilization or Barbarism*, US, Lawrence Hill Books, 1991, pp.283-284.

Charles S. Finch, *Africa and the birth of science and technology: A brief overview*, US, Khenti, 1992, pp.13-17

Charles S. Finch, *Science and Symbol in Egyptian Medicine: Commentaries on the Edwin Smith Papyrus*, from *Egypt Revisited*, edited by Ivan Van Sertima, US, Transaction Publishers, 1989, pp.325-351

Charles S. Finch, *The African Background of Medical Science*, from *Blacks in Science: Ancient and Modern*, edited by Ivan Van Sertima, US, Transaction Publishers, 1983, pp.140-147

Frederick Newsome, *Black Contributions to the Early History of Medicine,* from *Blacks in Science: Ancient and Modern,* edited by Ivan Van Sertima, US, Transaction Publishers, 1983, pp.127-139

Théophile Obenga, *African Philosophy: The Pharaonic Period: 2780-330 BC,* Senegal, Per Ankh, 2004, pp.371-381, 400, 412-414, 418-420

Chapter 4: Navigation and Cartography

Charles S. Finch, *The Star of Deep Beginnings,* US, Khenti, 1998, pp.206-220.

Charles Hapgood, *Maps of the Ancient Sea Kings,* US, Chilton Book Co., 1966, whole book

R. A. Jairazbhoy, *Ancient Egyptians and Chinese in America,* UK, George Prior Associated Publishers, 1974, whole book

Rafique Jairazbhoy, *Rameses III: Father of Ancient America,* UK, Karnak House, 1992, whole book

Ivan Van Sertima ed, *African Presence in Early America,* US, Transaction Publishers, 1992, pp.5-163

Ivan Van Sertima, *Early America Revisited,* US, Transaction Publishers, 1998, pp.31-197

Count Alexander Von Wuthenau, *Art of the World: Pre-Columbian Terracottas,* UK, Methuen & Co., 1969, whole book

Chapter 5: Architecture

Nnamdi Elleh, *African Architecture: Evolution and Transformation,* US, McGraw-Hill, 1997, pp.22-41

Charles S. Finch, *The Star of Deep Beginnings,* US, Khenti, 1998, pp.101-135

Dietrich Wildung, *Egypt from Prehistory to the Romans,* Germany, Taschen, 1997, pp.7-165

Chapter 6: Others

Hunter Havelin Adams III, *African & African-American Contributions to Science and Technology,* US, Portland Baseline Essay, 1986, pp.39, 51, 54 and Figure 28

Charles S. Finch, *The Star of Deep Beginnings,* US, Khenti, 1998, pp.28-30, 35-38, 48

Gamal Mokhtar, *Official Statement on the Messiha Discovery,* from *Blacks in Science: Ancient and Modern,* edited by Ivan Van Sertima, US, Transaction Publishers, 1983, pp.97-98

Théophile Obenga, *Ancient Egypt & Black Africa,* UK, Karnak House, 1992, pp.102-103

PART TWO

THE MYSTERIOUS SCIENCES OF THE GREAT PYRAMID

PREFACE

The Great Pyramid of Giza is a monument of such scientific importance that I have made that building the sole subject matter for the second part of this book. Standing at the height of a forty storey building, it was, as late as the nineteenth century, the tallest building in the world. Of the Seven Wonders of the Ancient World, it remains the sole survivor.

Peter Lemesurier, an author of a number of radical and mystical books, wrote:

> For over 40 centuries the Great Pyramid of Giza in Egypt has tantalised and baffled mankind. Is it a royal tomb, a treasure-house, a temple of initiation, an astronomical observatory, a mathematician's folly, or an incredibly sophisticated public-works project necessitated by the state of the ancient Egyptian economy? Or is it, as some persist in believing, nothing less than the Bible itself, written in solid stone? Or is it, again, a kind of 'time-capsule'--a code message from some ancient civilisation of which we know nothing, perhaps immeasurably older even than Egypt itself?

Historians influenced by Herodotus, the erudite Greek historian, painted a lurid picture of a despotic ruler forcing thousands of oppressed workers to build a monument to satisfy an oversized ego. Herodotus even reported that in Egyptian tradition, Cheops, the Pharaoh who commissioned the monument, was remembered as a figure of hate who oppressed the Egyptian people. How true was any of this?

Other writers have addressed the technological and scientific implications of the monument. Beginning with the Arab conquerors of Egypt in the early Middle Ages, and continuing up to our own times, survey after survey has been conducted on the Great Pyramid. Some were designed to find passageways into the building to find treasure. Others were to test mathematical and geodetic theories to see if the Egyptian builders possessed high scientific knowledge. What were their findings? What do these surveys tell us about the state of early African science and technology? Is it true that the Great Pyramid encompasses high mathematical and scientific knowledge?

Much of the scholarly literature on the Great Pyramid, however, had problems that must be addressed. Some research suffered from the fact that the earlier authors were often highly religious and spiritual people who studied the Great Pyramid with the express intention to prove that the Egyptians had highly mystical knowledge which, among other things, proved certain Biblical prophecies correct. Other books were way too technical or mathematical for the ordinary reader.

Perhaps the best single work on the subject is *Secrets of the Great Pyramid* by Peter Tompkins (US, Harper & Row, 1978). It remains a work of impressive scholarship, however, I believe that some the ideas in the book could be simplified and presented in a bite-sized form. To that end, I wrote a lecture essay on the Great Pyramid in 2010 and then an e-book in 2011. The lecture essay and e-book formed the basis of the text that you are reading right here.

CHAPTER ONE: INTRODUCING THE GREAT PYRAMID

Historians are generally concerned with the 'what,' the 'where,' the 'when,' and the 'by whom.'

What is the Great Pyramid of Giza?

The Great Pyramid of Giza is one of the most important man-made structures in the world. It is a key tourist attraction for the modern nation of Egypt. Its size, design, attributes, and technical complexity have fascinated scholars for many years. Myths and legends have surrounded its construction. Many have pondered over its purpose.

It is interesting to get an opinion on the Great Pyramid. This is what Walter Marsham Adams wrote about this monument over a hundred years ago:

Figure 28. The Great Pyramid of Giza.

The Monument in stone is unique, solid almost to indestructibility, incapable of variation, and standing unchanged and unchanging, regardless of the assaults, whether of time or of man. That extraordinary pile, the most majestic and most mysterious ever erected by the hand of man, stands close to the verge of the immense desert which stretches its arid wastes across the whole breadth of the African continent to the shore of the western ocean, just at the spot where the busy life of the earliest civilisation on record was bordered by the vast and barren solitude. Of all the other structures which made the marvels of the ancient world, scarcely a vestige is left. Where are the hanging gardens, the boast of the monarch of Babylon? Where is the far-famed Pharos of Alexandria? Centuries have passed since earthquake laid low the Colossus which bestrode the harbour of Rhodes; and a madman's hand reduced to ashes the temple of Artermis, the pride of Ephesus. But the Grand Pyramid of Ghizeh [sic] still remains, undestroyed and indestructible, ages after the lesser marvels have passed away, as it stood ages before ever they came into being.

Where is the Great Pyramid of Giza located?

The monument is located in the desert area of northern Egypt. Strangely enough, some of the construction materials are thought to have come from Aswan located some 500 miles away near the Egyptian and Nubian border.

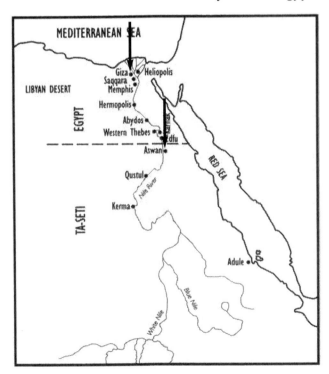

Figure 29. Map of Ancient Egypt and Nubia showing the location of Giza and Aswan.

When was the Great Pyramid of Giza built?

There is general agreement that the Great Pyramid was constructed during the time of the second or third ruler of the Fourth Egyptian Dynasty.

However, the actual dating of this, and most other periods in Egyptian history, remains controversial indeed. No doubt, you may have seen dates such as 2600 or 2500 BC appearing in books and internet articles for the building of the Great Pyramid, but you should not be fooled by the apparent unanimity of the different sources. What has happened here is that the scholars and the popularisers have agreed to use a chronology derived from the ideas of Professor Eduard Meyer (1887) and his student Professor James Henry Breasted (1906), see below.

According to this view, the First Dynasty began to rule Egypt before 3000 BC. This is more than five thousand years ago. If this is true, then it is likely that the Fourth Dynasty ruled around 2600 or 2500 BC. This is more than four thousand five hundred years ago. This is said to give us a date of 2600 or 2500 BC for the building of the Great Pyramid.

However, the Meyer-Breasted chronology is deeply flawed and accommodates only a fraction of the known documentary clues that would ordinarily be used to create an Egyptian timeline. In addition, their timeline has not convinced scholars who have actually checked the chronological data for themselves. It has only convinced those who haven't or those who cannot construct logically consistent arguments.

Below, I present a table of the chronological ideas of various authorities beginning with the Ancient Egyptian historian, Manetho, writing in the third century BC. The biggest differences between the authorities are in the estimations of the First, the Twelfth, and the Eighteenth Egyptian dynasties.

	DYNASTIES (Dates are BC)			
	I	VI	XII	XVIII
Manetho (3rd century BC)	5717	4426	3440	1674
Wilkinson (1836)	2320			1575
Champollion-Figeac (1839)	5867	4426	3703	1822
Lepsius (1858)	3892	2744	2380	1591
Brugsch (1877)	4400	3300	2466	1700
Meyer (1887)	3180	2530	2130	1530
Breasted (1906)	3400	2625	2000	1580
Petrie (1906)	5510	4206	3459	1580
Petrie (1929)	4553	3282	2586	1587
MacNaughton (1932)	5776	4360	3389	1709
Pochan (1971)	5619	4326	3336	1595

Brunson & Rashidi (1989)	3200	2345	1991	1560
Rohl (1998)	2789	2224	1800	1193
Chinweizu (1999)	4443	3162	1994	1788
Author (2006)	*5660*	*4402*	*3405*	*1709*

My chronology is similar to that of Manetho, and is also similar to the chronological timelines constructed by Sir Flinders Petrie (1906), Duncan MacNaughton (1932), and Professor André Pochan (1971). Our chronologies would place the Fourth Dynasty around 4800 BC. This is a mind boggling six thousand eight hundred years ago!

Other scholars, such as the great Nigerian intellectual, Professor Chinweizu, try to sit on the fence alongside Brugsch (1877).

Who built the Great Pyramid of Giza?

There is general agreement that Pharaoh Khufu commissioned the Great Pyramid. However, there is a controversial nineteenth century visitor, Colonel Howard Vyse, who presented data that contradicts this. He claimed to have seen and copied hieroglyphic characters from inside the Great Pyramid which, when read correctly, are for a certain Pharaoh 'Rafu'. I do not know who 'Rafu' is, and nor does anyone else. Other scholars have accused Vyse of fabricating this data.

Which ever be the case, Khufu is also called Cheops by Greek historians, Khnum-Khuf in some of the old inscriptions and Suphis I by Manetho. He was the second (some say third) ruler of the Fourth Dynasty. This ruling family were of Memphite or Elephantine origins (i.e. the family came from Memphis, the Egyptian capital, or from Elephantine, on the Egyptian Nubian border).

I think that there were seven rulers of the Fourth Dynasty, and I date them as follows, listing Khufu as the second king (ruled 4824-4761 BC):

4872 - 4824	Sneferu
4824 - 4761	*Khufu*
4761 - c.4744	Djedefra
4744 - 4678	Khafra
4678 - 4615	Menkaura
4615 - 4608	Shepseskaf
4608 - 4599	Thampthis

The Great Pyramid may well have been built after the thirtieth year of his reign, which might be after 4794 BC.

The Mysterious Sciences of the Great Pyramid

Figure 30. Ivory statuette of Pharaoh Khufu showing a distinctly African profile.

CHAPTER TWO: WHAT WAS INVOLVED IN BUILDING THE GREAT PYRAMID?

The Great Pyramid was composed of 2.3 million blocks of stone, arranged into 210 courses of masonry. This raises one difficult question: How do you raise 210 courses towards a point without the building twisting as you build?

The average weight of the interior blocks was 2.5 tons, with a range of 1 to 7 tons. Some of the casing stones at the base weigh 16 tons. The granite blocks in the King's Chamber weigh 100 tons. Even more amazing is the fact that these granite blocks came from Aswan, which is 500 miles south.

How did the Ancient Egyptians organise all of this?

The most important early discussion of this question comes from the writings of Herodotus, the Ancient Greek historian. According to him, the Great Pyramid took 30 years to build. They spent the first 10 years building the causeway and the final 20 years building the monument. Apparently, the workers were arranged into shifts of 100,000 labourers at a time. The workmen were fed radishes, onions and garlic.

The building of the monument required vast project management abilities. The planners would have to factor in the possibilities of accidents and emergencies. They would have to ensure that each worker was continuously employed in a variety of tasks. Some workers quarried the blocks, others transported them by sleds and watercraft sometimes to a distance of 500 miles, others assembled the blocks into the pyramidal shape with astounding accuracy challenged by the time constraint of positioning each block in 91.5 seconds (see below). The planners would have to check that the transportation was adequate, workers were fed and watered, sick relief was on hand, and their own planning teams could handle a task lasting 20 years. Also to be factored in is the housing, feeding and policing of at least 150,000 women and children in the settlements nearby. This is no small task!

Wayne Chandler, an African American historian, reports a calculation that 2.3 million blocks of stone divided by a 20 year period suggests that each block was in place every 91.5 seconds assuming a 12 hour work day.

The Mysterious Sciences of the Great Pyramid 63

Figure 31. Sketch showing remnants of the original limestone casing of the Great Pyramid. The limestone blocks originally covered the entire monument and the joints between the blocks were barely visible. During the Arab period, the limestone casing was largely stripped away to build their capital city of Cairo.

This seems very unlikely but no one has suggested a better explanation. It is still the case that no one knows how the pyramid was built.

2.3 million blocks of stone are, of course, an enormous number to handle. It is important to put this vast figure into perspective. According to Wayne Chandler: 'The Great Pyramid contains more stone than all the churches, chapels and cathedrals built in England since the time of Christ.' Mr Chandler gave a second example: 'If all the stone in the pyramid were sawed into blocks one foot on an edge and these were laid end to end, they would stretch two thirds of the way around the globe at the equator.' Finally: 'The Great Pyramid contains enough stone to construct thirty Empire State Buildings.'

The unusually high quality of the workmanship has attracted the interest of scholars. According to Sir Gaston Maspero, considered the greatest French Egyptologist of all time: the casing was 'so subtly jointed that one would have said that it was a single slab from top to bottom.' According to Sir Flinders Petrie, the brilliant and exacting British archaeologist: 'the mean thickness of the joints is 0.020 of an inch; and, therefore, the mean variation of the cutting of the stone from a straight line and from a true square is but 0.01 of an inch on a length of 75 inches up the face, an amount of accuracy equal to the most modern opticians' straight-edges of such a length.' Emphasising the point, Petrie also wrote: 'To merely place such stones in exact contact at the sides would be careful work, but to do so with cement in the joint seems almost impossible.'

What are the dimensions of the Great Pyramid?

It is difficult to accurately measure the dimensions of the Great Pyramid due to the fact that most of the limestone casing that once covered the monument has since been stripped away.

However, Robert Bauval and Graham Hancock, two contemporary scholars, report the following estimates based on a relatively recent survey of the building. The north side was found to be 755 feet, 4.8919 inches in length. The south side was found to be 756 feet, 0.9739 inches. The east side was found to be 755 feet, 10.4937 inches. The west side was found to be 755 feet, 9.1551 inches. Thus, the variation between the longest and the shortest sides is less than 8 inches, an error of only a tenth of a percent. This is astonishingly accurate considering that each side is 9000 inches long!

How accurate were the corners?

Robert Bauval and Graham Hancock report the following measurements: The north west corner of the Great Pyramid varied from 90 degrees by a miniscule 00'02", the north east corner by only 03'02", the south east corner by only 03'33" and the south west corner by only 00'33". Dr Alfred Russell Wallace, a most important British scientist, commented on this more than a hundred years ago in an address before the British Association for the Advancement of Science where he said the following: '1. That the pyramid is truly square, the sides being equal, and the angles right angles.'

Is it level?

According to Anthony Browder, an African American Egyptologist: 'The entire pyramid rests on a platform which is more than 755 feet in length, and level to within four-fifths of an inch.' Again, this is not a new revelation. Dr Alfred Russell Wallace in his address before the British Association for the Advancement of Science said: '2. That the four sockets

The Mysterious Sciences of the Great Pyramid

on which the first four stones of the corners rested are truly on the same level.'

What about its orientation?

It is well known that the Great Pyramid's sides are orientated to North, South, East and West. According to Bauval and Hancock: 'Less well known is just how eerily exact is the precision of these alignments--with the average deviation from true being only a little over 3 arc minutes (i.e. about 5 per cent of a single degree).' Again, to cite Dr Alfred Russell Wallace a third time: '3. That the directions of the sides are accurate to the four cardinal points.'

How high was the Pyramid?

The problem of calculation is particularly acute here. However, Bauval and Hancock report a figure of 481.3949 feet for the vertical height of the monument. That raised an interesting question: Was π built into the structure of the Pyramid?

John Taylor, a British journalist writing for the *London Observer,* wrote an 1864 book entitled *The Great Pyramid: Why was it built? & Who built it?* He discovered that if he divided the perimeter of the Pyramid by twice its height, it gave him a quotient of 3.144, i.e. close to the value of π.

CHAPTER THREE: MATHEMATICAL, ASTRONOMICAL, AND OTHER ENIGMAS

Bauval and Hancock report a figure of 3023.16 feet for the base perimeter of the Great Pyramid. They also report a figure of 481.3949 feet for the vertical height.

Since the radius of a circle x 2 = the diameter of a circle, and the diameter x π = the circumference of a circle, therefore π = the circumference divided by the diameter of a circle. Crunching some figures, this means: 481.3949 x 2 = 962.7898. Therefore π = 3023.16/962.7898 = 3.14. Compare this figure with the more accurate modern figure of 3.14159 to 5 decimal places. According to Dr Alfred Russell Wallace: '4. That the vertical height of the pyramid bears the same proportion to its circumference at the base as the radius of a circle does to its circumference.'

Was the Pyramid symbolic of the northern hemisphere?

According to Bauval and Hancock:

> Equally 'impossible' ... is the relationship, in a scale of 1:43,200, that exists between the dimensions of the Pyramid and the dimensions of the earth ... it is a simple fact, verifiable on any pocket calculator, that if you take the monument's original height (481.3949 feet) and multiply this by 43,200 you get a quotient of 3938.685 miles. This is an underestimate by just 11 miles of the true figure for the polar radius of the earth (3949 miles) ... Likewise, if you take the monument's perimeter at the base (3023.16 feet) and multiply this figure by 43,200 then you get 24,734.94 miles--a result that is within 170 miles of the true equatorial circumference of the earth (24,902 miles).

Clearly Bauval and Hancock seem impressed by this coincidence. I am less convinced for one simple reason. Any spherical object (including a snooker ball, a tennis ball, or even a football) could be scaled up by a particular ratio to give the approximate dimensions of the earth! Consequently, I believe much more evidence is required to support the Bauval and Hancock assertion. Fortunately, I believe that such evidence may exist. Walter Marsham Adams presented the following data in an Appendix to his book:

DISTANCE FROM POLE IS EQUAL TO DISTANCE FROM CENTRE. PAGE 54

This property may perhaps be clear from the following considerations. Suppose C to be the centre of the earth, P the situation of the Great Pyramid, N the North Pole, and E the point where the meridian of the building cuts the equator, then E C P will be the latitude of the building, viz., 30°, whence it will be seen at once that the triangle C N P will be equilateral, since the angle at C is 60°, and the radii C N and C P will be equal to each other, assuming the earth to be a sphere. 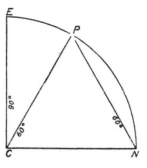 Hence therefore P N, the distance from the Pyramid to the North Pole, will be equal to P C, the distance to the centre of the earth.

However, Adams assumed that the world is perfectly spherical but in fact it isn't. The poles are slightly flattened.

However, the actual latitude of the Pyramid is not exactly 30 degrees. It is actually 29 degrees 58'51". This may indicate that placing the Pyramid slightly below 30 degrees was deliberate. Moreover, it would make the Pyramid close to equidistant between the centre of the earth and the North Pole!

But surely, this is just a fluke?

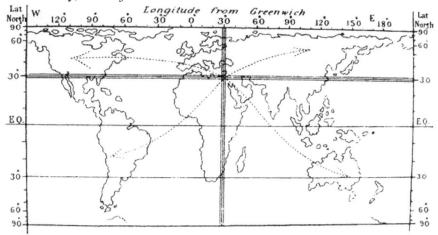

Figure 32. Drawing a longitudinal line through the Great Pyramid passes through more north-south land mass than any other longitude. Similarly, a latitudinal line through the Great Pyramid passes through more east-west land mass than any other latitude.

How about this?

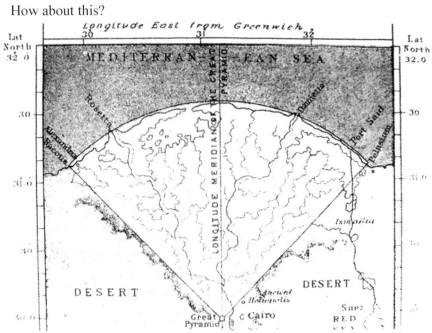

Figure 33. Drawing a meridian line through the position of the Great Pyramid bisects the Delta into two equal triangular areas.

But surely, the Ancient Egyptians chose any suitable flat ground to build on?

Surely it is just a coincidence that the location bisects the Delta into two equal triangular sectors? Surely it is just a coincidence that the longitudinal line passes through the most north-south land mass and the latitudinal line passes through the most east-west landmass?

Bauval and Hancock present solid reasons why the location was not chosen arbitrarily:

> And what makes this miracle all the more remarkable is the fact that it was not performed on a perfectly flat area of ground, as one might expect, but with a massive natural mound, or hill, left exactly in the middle of the site ... Estimated to be almost 30 feet--as tall as a two-storey house--and positioned dead centre over the base area (of which it occupies approximately 70 per cent), this primeval mound was skilfully incorporated into lower courses of the growing edifice.

If the Great Pyramid really was symbolic of the size of earth, why pick such an arbitrary size?

The Great Pyramid is 755.5 feet against 481.3 feet which seems an arbitrary size to choose. However, the Egyptians actually reckoned the base as 440 royal cubits (half the base was 220 royal cubits), the vertical height as 280 royal cubits, and the sloping height as 356 royal cubits. Thus the Egyptians thought of the Great Pyramid's dimensions in round numbers. The evidence that the Great Pyramid was built using the royal cubit as a standard of measurement is solid. Peter Tompkins narrated the story of how Sir Isaac Newton demonstrated this fact in the eighteenth century. Newton called the royal cubit the 'profane cubit' and suggested that its use originated in the Ancient Egyptian city of Memphis. Newton's idea could be confirmed. Tompkins mentions that a Nilometer in Elephantine was discovered that confirmed the use of this unit of measure.

Peter Lemesurier lists 30 examples from inside the Pyramid that are clearly based on the royal cubit. For example, the Descending Passage inside the Pyramid is 2 royal cubits in width. The pit section of the Great Subterranean Chamber is 2 royal cubits in depth. The Ascending Passage is 2 royal cubits in width. Lemesurier reports speculation that the original length of the Granite Plug was 10 royal cubits. The Queens Chamber Passage is 2 royal cubits in width throughout and the height of the downward step at the beginning of the second portion of it was 1 royal cubit.

The Queen's Chamber itself contained several measurements that used the royal cubit. The width of the niche at the top from north to south was 1 royal cubit, the depth of the niche from east to west was 2 royal cubits, the east-west distance from the Queen's Chamber Passage axis to the north-south niche axis was 2 royal cubits, the width of the niche at the bottom from north to south was 3 royal cubits, the width of the Chamber itself from north to south was 10 royal cubits, and the length of the Chamber from east to west was 11 royal cubits.

Lemesurier on page 301 of his book gave the length of the royal cubit as 20.63 inches and states that actual measuring sticks of this length have survived.

The measurements of the Queen's Chamber were important for another reason. The north-south distance from the Queens Chamber axis to the East West niche axis is 25.0265 inches in length. According to Peter Lemesurier, this measurement appears two more times inside the Great Pyramid and two more times outside the Great Pyramid. This measurement is known as the 'sacred cubit' and its importance in the building of the Great Pyramid has led to many acrimonious debates. The reason for the controversy is that this measurement multiplied by 10 million (= 250,265,000 inches) is a good approximation of the distance from the North Pole to the centre of the earth! Lemesurier gives the correct figure as 250,265,030.4 inches. I am less convinced, however. Why are there 30 internal examples of measurements based on the royal cubit but only three alleged measurements based on the sacred cubit? I have never seen a convincing explanation of why this is.

Moreover, Lemesurier was of the opinion that the Egyptians had a unit of measurement called the Pyramid or primitive inch which was 1.00106 inches. However, the evidence that the Egyptians ever had such a measurement has NOT BEEN ESTABLISHED. Lemesurier lists 14 examples where this measurement was used internally in the Great Pyramid on pages 330 and 331 of his book. In eight of these cases even he admits that the measurements are only approximate or are mean measurements. I am of the opinion that the deductions based on this unit of measurement do not stand up. I have, therefore, excluded them from this paper.

Why were the dimensions of the Pyramid specifically chosen?

Scholars have put forward two theories that may explain the size and scale of the Pyramid. One theory derives from the original writings of the Greek scholar Agarthachides. His works have not survived but other Classical writers quoted and paraphrased him. According to Professor Livio Stecchini, a professor of the History of Science, Agarthachides reported that each side of the Great Pyramid was the same length as 1/8 of a minute of a degree. This suggests that the four sides of the Pyramid were the same length as 1/2 of a minute of a degree. What does this mean? Mathematicians divide a circle into 360 degrees. Each degree can be subdivided into 60 portions called minutes. Thus 1/2 a minute of a degree is 1/180 of a degree.

If the four sides of the Pyramid represent the northern hemisphere, then the perimeter of the Pyramid must represent the equator. Professor Stecchini reported that the perimeter of the Pyramid was 921.453 metres. However, Peter Tomkins reported that 1/2 a minute of latitude of the earth at the equator is 1,842.9/2 = 921.45 metres. This is almost exactly the same figure! The exactitude is scarily close.

However, there is another theory. There are 5,280 feet in a mile, therefore 481.3949 feet, the height of the Pyramid, equals 0.0911732 miles. This is calculated as 481.3949/5280 = 0.0911732. Is there any significance to this number? It is approximately 1/1,000,000,000th the average distance from the earth to the sun, where 0.0911732 x 1,000,000,000 = 91,173,200. The truer figure of the earth to the sun is thought to vary from 91 to 94.5 million miles. Clearly 1,000,000,000 is a round number and would thus suggest that the dimensions of the Great Pyramid were not chosen arbitrarily.

So the issues are these: Was Agarthachides correct to report that each side of the Pyramid was built to represent 1/8 of a minute of a degree? If so, this suggests that the Egyptians are the founders of the degree and the minute. It may also suggest that the apparent relationship between the height of the Pyramid and the distance to the sun is just the result of luck. Are other scholars correct to say the Pyramid's size was chosen to represent the average distance between the earth and the sun? If so, this suggests that Egyptian astronomy was particularly well advanced. It may also suggest that the relationship between the size of the Pyramid and the size of the equator is just the result of luck.

There is another possibility, however. Were the Egyptians attempting to do BOTH THINGS AT ONCE? Were they attempting to simultaneously show a relationship between the earth and the sun AND the Pyramid and the earth's equator?

What is the Golden Section?

In the year 1202, Fibonacci learned of the 'rabbits problem' while in North Africa, i.e. Egypt and Algiers. Fibonacci popularised an imaginary set of ideal conditions under which rabbits could breed, and posed the question: 'How many pairs of rabbits will there be a year from now?'

The ideal conditions were as follows:

1. You begin with one male rabbit and one female rabbit. These rabbits have just been born.
2. A rabbit will reach sexual maturity after one month.
3. The gestation period of a rabbit is one month.
4. Once she has reached sexual maturity, a female rabbit will give birth every month.
5. A female rabbit will always give birth to one male rabbit and one female rabbit.
6. The rabbits never die.

Crunching some figures for the 'rabbits problem', we get the following:
* At the beginning, there is one pair of rabbits.
* After one month, the two rabbits have mated but have not given birth. Therefore, there is still only one pair of rabbits.
* After 2 months, the first pair of rabbits gives birth to another pair, making two pairs in total.
* After 3 months, the original pair gives birth again, and the second pair mate, but do not give birth. This makes three pairs in total.
* After 4 months, the original pair gives birth, and the pair born in month 2 give birth. The pair born in month 3 mate, but do not give birth. This makes two new pairs, or five pairs in total.
* After 5 months, every pair that was alive two months ago gives birth. This makes three new pairs, or eight pairs in total.

The sequence of numbers becomes 1, 1, 2, 3, 5, 8 ... also 13, 21, 34, 55, 89, 144, 233, etc. Note also that 233/144 = 1.6180555, 144/89 = 1.61797 and 89/55 = 1.618181. Compare these numbers with *phi* or φ = 1.618 to 3 decimal places.

Why is this important? So what?

This figure, 1.618 to 3 decimal places, is also called the Golden Section (the actual figure, like π, is an irrational number of infinite decimal places). Snail's shells are based on this number. Artists and architects have found that if they base their designs on this number, the results are often aesthetically pleasing. It has even been claimed that a beautiful human face is also based on this figure.

Herodotus reported information on the Great Pyramid that has led to another lively and acrimonious debate amongst scientists and mathematicians. One web page, *EXTERNAL DIMENSIONS OF THE GREAT PYRAMID*, credibly quotes the great Greek historian as writing: 'the sides of the great pyramid are 8 plethra and the height is the same.' What does this mean? The same page explains:

> In ancient Greece, plethra denoted both a linear measure of 100 Greek feet and a square measure of one acre ... The statement that the sides and the height of the pyramid are 8 plethra is based on an ancient Egyptian acre.

Professor Herbert W. Turnbull, a distinguished mathematician and author of *The Great Mathematicians*, was perhaps the first to give the Herodotus passage this explanation. He wrote:

The Mysterious Sciences of the Great Pyramid

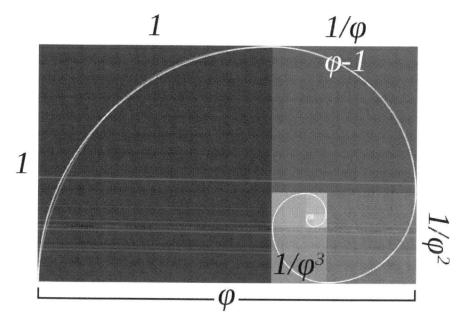

Figure 34. Diagram showing the relationship between 1 and *phi* i.e. 1.618 (to 3 decimal places). Notice how these numbers can be used to model a snail's shell.

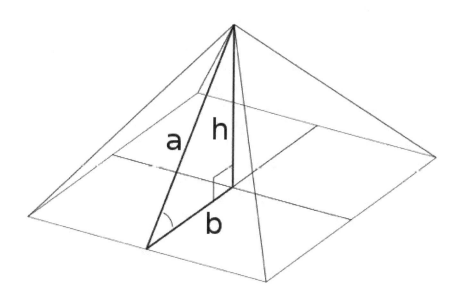

Figure 35. Line 'a' is the sloping height of the Pyramid. It is 356 cubits in length.

> A certain obscure passage in Herodotus can, by the slightest literal emendation, be made to yield excellent sense. It would imply that the area of each triangular face of the Pyramid is equal to the square of the vertical height and this accords well with the actual facts. If this be so, the ratios of height, slope and base can be expressed in terms of the Golden Section.

Is this the correct explanation? Scholars who oppose this idea claim instead that Herodotus meant to convey that each side of the monument was 800 Greek feet in length. Moreover, the Pyramid was 800 Greek feet tall. Most of the translators of the Herodotus passage follow this second interpretation.

There is one obvious problem with this perspective, however. The Pyramid is clearly NOT 800 feet tall. If it was, each face of the monument would look much more like a narrow isosceles triangle. Since the monument clearly does not have this shape, this interpretation cannot explain how Herodotus could have come by this figure. This interpretation is therefore unlikely.

On the other hand, Peter Tompkins, convinced that Herodotus was speaking of acres, gave the area of each triangular side of the Pyramid as 78,320 royal cubits. He calculated this using the basic formula for the area of a triangle (i.e. base x height)/2. Crunching the numbers, (440 x 356)/2 = 78,320 square cubits. In addition, Tompkins points about that 78,320 square cubits is close to 78,400 square cubits. Why is this significant? The height of the Pyramid is 280 royal cubits. If this figure was squared it becomes 78,400 square cubits. What do these figures have to do with Herodotus' idea that the sides of the Pyramid and its height were 8 plethra or acres?

The web page, *EXTERNAL DIMENSIONS OF THE GREAT PYRAMID*, claim that one acre equals 9,800 square cubits. Therefore eight acres is 9,800 x 8 which equals 78,400 square cubits. Tompkins, like Professor Turbull before him, believes that this is a truer rendering of the cryptic passage that Herodotus wrote. Herodotus was attempting to convey the idea that the area of each side of the Pyramid (7.9918 acres or 78,320 square cubits) approximately equals the height of the Pyramid squared (8 acres or 78,400 square cubits). If this is the correct interpretation, crunching the numbers lend support to Professor Turbull's idea that the Golden Section WAS deliberately built into the structure. Here is how.

Let us crunch some figures. If the sloping height of the Pyramid is 356 royal cubits and half of the base is 220, then 356/220 = 1.61818181. Compare 1.61818181 with $\varphi = 1.618$ to 3 decimal places.

The Mysterious Sciences of the Great Pyramid 75

But surely this is just another coincidence?

It has been suggested by some critics that the Ancient Egyptian architects merely liked the pleasing aesthetic effects provided by π and the Golden Section but probably had no idea that they were in fact irrational numbers. However, the evidence provided by Professor Beatrice Lumpkin shown on page 14 of this book provides evidence, regarded as convincing by many scholars, that the Ancient Egyptians were perfectly familiar with irrational numbers. By comparing the two key Egyptian measures the royal cubit and the double remen, Lumpkin shows that a double remen is equal to the square root of 2 cubits. In mathematics, the square root of 2 is regarded as THE irrational number *par excellence*.

Finally: Was the Great Pyramid used to pinpoint the Spring Equinox?

The Spring Equinox is the day of the year, March 21, where the day and night are of equal length being 12 hours each. Professor André Pochan points out that on the day of the Spring Equinox at both 6 AM and 6 PM the sun causes a rapid movement of light against the Pyramid's southern face. At 12 o'clock midday on the Spring Equinox, the Pyramid also swallows its shadow.

Is this yet another coincidence?

CHAPTER FOUR: STRAIGHT OUT OF LEFT FIELD

M. Bovis, a Frenchman, noticed that some bins inside the King's Chamber contained dead cats and other small animals that had wandered into the Pyramid and died. Strangely enough, the dead animals had no smell of decay. Bovis examined the animals and found them to have dehydrated and mummified.

He conducted his own experiments with dead cats, and calf's brains with his own model pyramid. These too failed to putrefy.

Karel Drbal, a Czechoslovakian engineer, tested Bovis' ideas and made a radical conclusion. He suggested that there is 'a definite relation between the shape of the space inside the pyramid, and the physical, chemical and biological processes going on inside that space.' Drbel conducted his own experiments using a used razor blade. After placing a used blade in his own model pyramid, it automatically recovered its sharpness. He could shave with one Gilette blue blade as many as 200 times.

He received patent number 91304 from the Czechoslovak patent office and began manufacturing 'Cheops Pyramid Razorblade Sharpeners' out of cardboard.

The Mystery of the Sarcophagus

The sarcophagus of Pharaoh Khufu must have been placed inside the King's Chamber before the monument was roofed because it is too large to pass through the entrance passage. This indicates that it was carved INSIDE the Pyramid.

According to Sir Flinders Petrie: 'Truth to tell, modern drill cores cannot hold a candle to the Egyptians ... their fine work shows the marks of such tools as we have only now reinvented.' This raises a key question that we address in the remainder of this section: What tools?

Mainstream Egyptologists attempt to explain this by claiming that the Ancient Egyptians only had copper tools. This is nonsense. As one engineer, Christopher Dunn, put it: To claim that copper tools can cut granite is like claiming that butter can cut aluminium!

The Mysterious Sciences of the Great Pyramid 77

Figure 36. The Sarcophagus in the King's Chamber.

Christopher Dunn says the following about himself:

> I'm not an Egyptologist, I'm a technologist. I do not have much interest in who died when, whom they may have taken with them and where they went to. No lack of respect is intended for the mountain of work and millions of hours of study conducted on this subject by intelligent scholars (professional and amateur), but my interest, thus my focus, is elsewhere.

He continues:

> When I look at an artifact [sic] to investigate how it was manufactured, I am not concerned about its history or chronology. Having spent most of my career

working with machinery that actually creates modern artifacts, such as jet-engine components, I'm able to analyze and determine how an artifact was created.

To give an example, Sir Flinders Petrie (who also had an engineering background) wrote the following over a hundred years ago:

> On the N. end (of the coffer) is a place, near the west side, where the saw was run too deep into the granite, and was backed out again by the masons; but this fresh start they made still too deep, and two inches lower and they backed out a second time, having cut out more than 0.10 of an inch deeper than they had intended.

Christopher Dunn addressed this as follows:

> When I read Petrie's passage concerning these deviations, a flood of memories came to me of my own history with saws, both power and manually driven. With these experiences, plus those observed in others, it seems inconceivable to me that manpower was the motivating force behind the saw which cut the granite coffers. While cutting steel with hand saws, an object that has a long workface, and certainly one with such dimensions as the coffers, would not be cut with great rapidity, and the direction the saw may turn can be seen well in advance of a serious mistake they made, the smaller the workpiece, naturally, the faster a blade would cut through it. On the other hand, if the saw is mechanised and is cutting rapidly through the workpiece, the saw could 'wander' from its intended course and cut through the guidance at a certain point at such a speed that the error is made before the condition can be corrected, this is not uncommon.

To give a second example, Sir Flinders Petrie wrote:

> On the E. inside is a portion of a tube-drill hole remaining, where they had tilted the drill over into the side by not working it vertically. They tried hard to polish away all that part, and took off about 1/10 of an inch thickness all around it; but still they had to leave the side of the hole 1/10 deep, three long, and 1.3 wide.

Christopher Dunn addressed this as follows:

> The errors noted by Petrie are not uncommon in modern machine shops, and I must confess to having made them myself on occasion. Several factors could be involved in creating this condition, although I cannot visualize any one of them being a hand operation. Once again, while working their drill into the granite, the machinists had made a mistake before they had time to correct it.

On the basis of this, Mr Dunn raises some interesting questions on what types of advanced machine tool technologies the Ancient Egyptians may

The Mysterious Sciences of the Great Pyramid 79

have possessed. Clearly they had technologies far in advance of the mere man power assumed by mainstream Egyptologists.

Summing Up

The findings in this essay show that the science and technology behind the Great Pyramid of Giza deserves much more mainstream attention. The specialists on Ancient Egypt have largely deserted this field and have left the research in the hands of the alternative scholars. However, Peter Tomkins and Professor Stecchini have shown that the alternative scholars have produced academic gold even when some of their findings are surrounded by dross. It is easy to separate one from the other.

I will give the final word to Peter Lemesurier. Even though I disagree with most of the findings in his book, *The Great Pyramid Decoded*, he does however present hard scientific evidence that must be considered seriously, quite apart from his esoteric Christian-based speculations. In his own words:

> It is one thing to align your building exactly with the earth's four cardinal points. It is quite another to site it at the exact centre of the geometrical quadrant formed by the Nile Delta--the ancient kingdom of Lower Egypt. And yet such was the case ... Reference to any equal-area projection of the earth's surface reveals that the chosen site also lies on the longest land-contact meridian on the earth's surface and at the geographical centre of its whole land mass including the Americas and Antarctica ... Meanwhile further measurements appear to give ... the mean distance of the earth from the sun ... If one wished to have an architectural symbol for the planet earth itself one could scarcely do better than to take the Great Pyramid of Giza ... And it turns out that the ratio of base-perimeter to height is none other than twice the quantity pi (π)—in other words, the Pyramid's height is to its base perimeter as a circle's radius is to its circumference ... The Pyramid's geometry, in other words, not only combines all the above data into a single, elegant identification of the planet upon which we live; it also gives these quantities durable expression *in terms of each other.*

BIBLIOGRAPHY

Preface

Peter Lemesurier, *The Great Pyramid Decoded*, UK, Element Books, 1977, back cover

Chapter 1: Introducing the Great Pyramid

W. Marsham Adams, *The Book of the Master*, 1898 (reprint US, ECA Associates, 1990), pp.105-106

Robert Bauval and Graham Hancock, *Keeper of Genesis*, UK, Mandarin, 1996, pp.106-111

Wayne Chandler, *Of Gods and Men: Egypt's Old Kingdom* in *Egypt Revisited*, edited by Ivan Van Sertima, US, Transaction Publishers, 1989, pp.118-120 and pp.145-154

John Jackson, *Man, God, and Civilization*, US, Citadel Press, 1972, pp.218-219

Chapter 2: What was involved in building the Great Pyramid?

Robert Bauval and Graham Hancock, *Keeper of Genesis*, UK, Mandarin, 1996, pp.38-44

Anthony T. Browder, *Nile Valley Contribution to Civilization*, US, Institute of Karmic Guidance, 1992, pp.103-111

Wayne Chandler, *Of Gods and Men: Egypt's Old Kingdom* in *Egypt Revisited*, edited by Ivan Van Sertima, US, Transaction Publishers, 1989, pp.145-154

Charles S. Finch, *The Star of Deep Beginnings*, US, Khenti, 1998, pp.110-111

Peter Tompkins, *Secrets of the Great Pyramid*, US, Harper and Row, 1978, pp.233, 234

Dr Alfred Russell Wallace, *Address to British Association for the Advancement of Science,* in *British Association Report,* Glasgow Meeting, 1876, Part II, UK, Notices and Abstracts, 1877.

Chapter 3: Mathematical, Astronomical, and Other Enigmas

W. Marsham Adams, *The Book of the Master,* 1898 (reprint US, ECA Associates, 1990), p.197

Robert Bauval and Graham Hancock, *Keeper of Genesis,* UK, Mandarin, 1996, pp.38-44

EXTERNAL DIMENSIONS OF THE GREAT PYRAMID,
http://home.hiwaay.net/~jalison/gpdx.html

Charles S. Finch, *The Star of Deep Beginnings,* US, Khenti, 1998, pp.117, 124, 127

John Jackson, *Man, God, and Civilization,* US, Citadel Press, 1972, pp.220-223

Peter Lemesurier, *The Great Pyramid Decoded,* UK, Element Books, 1977, pp.6-11, 299-301, 327-332

Peter Tompkins, *Secrets of the Great Pyramid,* US, Harper and Row, 1978, pp.30-31, 47, 189-203

Herbert W. Turnbull is quoted on the webpage *The Golden Mean,* see http://community.middlebury.edu/~harris/Humanities/TheGoldenMean.html

Livio Catullo Stecchini, *Notes on the Relation of Ancient Measures to the Great Pyramid,* in *Secrets of the Great Pyramid,* by Peter Tompkins, US, Harper and Row, 1978, pp.363-372

Dr Alfred Russell Wallace, *Address to British Association for the Advancement of Science,* in *British Association Report,* Glasgow Meeting, 1876, Part II, UK, Notices and Abstracts, 1877.

Chapter 4: Straight out of left field

Christopher Dunn is quoted in David Hatcher Childress, *Technology of the Gods,* US, Adventures Unlimited, 2000, pp.264-272

Peter Lemesurier, *The Great Pyramid Decoded,* UK, Element Books, 1977, pp.6-11

Peter Tompkins, *Secrets of The Great Pyramid,* US, Harper & Row, 1978, pp.275-278

PART THREE

AFRICAN PROTO SCIENCE AND TECHNOLOGY

African Proto Science and Technology

PREFACE

Africa has a prehistory of proto scientific and technological endeavours on which the Ancient Egyptians built. Professor Yosef ben Jochannan in 1971 popularised in the Black communities the discovery of the 43,000 year old mine discovered in Swaziland. In a similar manner, Professor Ivan Van Sertima in 1983 popularised the discovery of prehistoric Nubian agriculture and 15,000 year old Kenyan animal husbandry. Professor Charles Finch in 1991 popularised the discovery of a 90,000 year old Congolese fishing based culture. However, in relaying this information, I have used terms like Swaziland, Nubia, Kenya, and Congo merely for geographical convenience. These countries did not, of course, exist back then! Dr Clyde-Ahmad Winters has long popularised the importance of the early Saharan cultures. Mr Fari Supiya in 2006 popularised the discovery of bladelet technology in central and southern Africa of between 182,000 and 74,000 years old.

New discoveries can add to our stock of knowledge or sometimes challenge previously held beliefs. For instance, the internet is awash with stories of the discovery in South Africa, of a stone built site some are calling Adam's Calendar.

In 2003 a South African aircraft pilot brought a discovery to the attention of the general public. Johan Heine flew over a megalithic site in Mpumalanga, South Africa. The site consists of a stone circle about 30 meters in diameter. The local elders call it 'The Birthplace of The Sun' or 'Inzalo y'Langa.' The pilot visited the monoliths and realized they were aligned to the cardinal points of north, south, east and west. Others were aligned to the equinoxes and solstices. Moreover, at least 3 monoliths were aligned towards the sunrise. Subsequent research revealed that the stones are all dolomite, weighing up to 5 tons each, and are thought to have been transported from a distant site. What did all this mean?

Bryan Hill wrote an article about this site where he said:

> The site is aptly named Adam's Calendar because the stones are placed to track the movement of the sun, which casts shadows on the rock. It still works

perfectly as a calendar today by following the shadow of the setting sun, which is cast by the taller central monolith onto the flat stone beside it.

How old was the site? Bryan Hill reported than an astronomer Bill Hollenbach suggested an age of at least 75,000 years. A further calculation performed in June 2009, suggested an age of at least 160,000 years. These ideas do indeed challenge preconceptions! However, in my book *When We Ruled,* I argued that the stone ruins of South Africa belonged to the mediaeval Munhumutapa Empire. I believe this information adds to our knowledge of the astronomy of mediaeval Munhumutapa. While I stand by this interpretation, however, I would be very delighted to be proved wrong. Imagine if Bill Hollenbach's dates stand up!

In this section, I shall give details of some of the different examples of proto scientific and proto technological endeavour in prehistoric Africa. I am not saying anything new. I am merely bringing together the research popularised by ben Jochannan, Van Sertima, Finch, Winters and Supiya.

AFRICAN PROTO SCIENCE AND TECHNOLOGY

Introduction

Professor Ivan Van Sertima suggests that the beginning of African proto scientific and technological endeavour is the domestication of fire 1,400,000 years ago near Lake Baringo in Kenya. The evidence of human control over fire comes from a site called Chesowanja. This is one million years before its first known appearance in China. *The New York Times* reported this as a front page story on November 14, 1981.

Tool Making

Fari Supiya reported archaeological finds of bladelet technology in Central East Africa and South Africa dating back to between 182,000 and 74,000 years old. Bladelets were small sharp tools made of stone. The Central East African and South African examples were harpoon points.

An example of these tools being used comes from an aquatic or fishing based culture in Katanda, a region in northeastern Congo 90,000 years ago. Alison Brooks of George Washington University and John Yellen of the National Science Foundation made the discovery in 1988. From the site they recovered a finely wrought series of harpoon points, all elaborately polished and barbed. Also uncovered was a tool, equally well crafted, believed to be a dagger. The Katanda people organised annual fishing expeditions during the rainy seasons. They caught catfish.

'What's exciting is that we're seeing strategic planning for subsistence by people who lived so long ago,' says Brooks. 'Humans in Africa invented sophisticated [tool] technologies long before their European counterparts, who have often been credited with initiating modern culture'.

Mining

Mining for hematite took place in Swaziland at Bomvu Ridge in the Ngwenya mountain range 43,200 years ago. In 1964 an iron-mining company, quite by accident, first made the discovery. Professor Raymond Dart, a scholar at the University of Witwatersrand in Johannesburg, made a scholarly study of the site. His team discovered a large cache of mining tools as well as tunnels and adits. This suggested that the prehistoric miners of this region were engaged in systematic mining. In time 300,000 artefacts were recovered including thousands of stonemade mining tools. The prehistoric miners dug for a metal called specularite. This is a type of hematite, an iron containing ore. Specularite comes in two distinct colours --red and black. Used as a cosmetic and a body dye, it may also have been used in funeral rituals.

Professor Dart was associated with another staggering discovery. In 1930 his archaeological team discovered a 28,000 years old manganese mine at Chowa in Zambia. They found thousands of prehistoric manganese tools, such as axes, chisels, choppers, grindstones, hammers and wedges. The miners probably used the manganese as a cosmetic because of the blackish colour of its ore. They also used it for tool making.

Proto Mathematics

How did humans in prehistoric times keep track of different days? An answer to this question emerged when excavations near Border Cave in the Lebombo Mountains between South Africa and Swaziland led to the recovery of a small piece of a baboon fibula. Dating from approximately 35,000 BC, and 7.7 cm long, this artefact was found to have been inscribed with 29 clearly defined notches.

Though 37,000 years old, some writers claim it resembles the calendar sticks still used by the San people of modern Namibia. Some think it represents a lunar phase counter suggesting that the proto-mathematicians who inscribed the notches were women using it to keep track on menstrual cycles. A menstrual cycle is approximately the same length as a lunar cycle. Other writers suggest that the bone demonstrated the existence of a refined accounting system that helped early humans to grasp the concept of time. The general importance cannot be overstated: The Lebombo Bone represents the first clear evidence of calculation in human history.

There are 30 spaces between and next to the 29 notches. One should read the spaces and notches as follows: 30 spaces plus 29 notches plus 30 spaces plus 29 notches plus 30 spaces, etcetera yields 30 29 30 29 30 ... nights. Moreover, the information could just as easily yield 30 59 89 118 148 177 207 236 266 295 325 354 nights for 1 2 3 4 5 6 7 8 9 10 11 12 lunations. A lunation is the average time of one lunar phase cycle. The length of any one lunar month can vary from 29.26 to 29.8 days. Most writers present it as approximately 29.5 days. Thus the Bone allows us to approximately calculate one lunation as 30 nights, two lunations as 59 nights (i.e. 30 + 29), three lunations as 89 nights (i.e. 30 + 29 + 30), four lunations as 118 nights (30 + 29 + 30 + 29), etcetera.

The Ishango bone is a 25,000 year old tool handle with notches carved into it. Jean de Heinzelin, a Belgian archaeologist of the Royal Institute of the Natural Sciences, unearthed it in the late 1950's. He excavated in the Ishango region of Congo near Lake Edward. On the tool are 3 rows of notches, two of which add up to sixty. The number patterns represented by the notches are of great interest.

Row 1 shows three notches carved next to six, four carved next to eight, ten carved next to two fives and finally a seven. The 3 and 6, 4 and 8, and 10 and 5, is believed to represent the process of doubling or 2n. Row 2 shows eleven notches carved next to twenty-one notches, and nineteen notches carved next to nine notches. This is thought to represent 10 + 1, 20 + 1, 20 - 1 and 10 - 1. Finally, Row 3 shows eleven notches, thirteen notches, seventeen notches and nineteen notches. 11, 13, 17 and 19 are the prime numbers between 10 and 20. A prime number can only be divided by itself and by 1 to produce a whole number.

The early mathematician(s?) behind the Ishango Bone therefore had some understanding of doubling or 2n, addition, subtraction and prime numbers.

CNN reported the Ishango evidence with great enthusiasm. Patricia Kelly, one of their reporters, said: 'It's thought Ishango Man's numbers system may have spread north following the River Nile into Egypt as well as into West Africa.'

Ishango is just four miles from Katanda, the site of the old harpoon-making culture. Moreover, Jean de Heinzelin discovered a cache of harpoon heads in Ishango, as well as the Ishango bone. De Heinzelin believed that the harpoonmaking culture diffused northward to the Nile Valley region from Ishango. Professor Finch quoted De Heinzelin as saying the following:

> From central Africa the [harpoon] style seems to have spread northward. At Khartoum near the upper Nile [in the Sudan] is a site that was occupied considerably later than Ishango. The harpoon points found show a diversity of styles ... [other harpoons] have the notches that seem to have been invented first at Ishango. Near Khartoum, at Es Shaheinab, is a Neolithic site that contains harpoon points bearing the imprint of Ishango ancestry; from here the Ishango technique moved westwards along the southern border of the Sahara ... The technology also seems to have followed a secondary branch northward

from Khartoum along the Nile Valley to Nagada in Egypt ... Other [Egyptian harpoons] show the influence of the Near Eastern Natufian culture [i.e. the prehistoric Negro culture of Palestine] and the Fayum [in Egypt] technique which is closely related to it.

Animal Husbandry and Agriculture

In 1980 Professor Charles Nelson, an anthropologist at the University of Massachusetts, announced an important find in the *New York Times*. Evidence had come to light of the domestication of cattle in Kenya 15,000 years ago. Dr Nelson's team found teeth and cattle bones spread over a limited area suggesting that the animals were not wild. Had the cattle been wild, the remains would have been more widely distributed over a larger area. Furthermore, evidence suggests that tsetse flies would have killed off any wild cattle. The highland regions where the cattle bones were discovered were generally free of flies, thus protecting them from this menace. Professor Nelson discovered the cattle bones at three sites in the Lukenya Hill District of the Kenyan highlands. The region was approximately 25 miles from Nairobi.

The first known advances in agriculture took place before 12,000 years ago. Professor Fred Wendorf and his colleagues discovered that Africans were the first to grow crops. In the floodplains of the Nile, now part of Egypt's Western Desert, the people of Wadi Kubbaniya cultivated crops of barley, capers, chickpeas, dates, legumes, lentils and wheat. Their ancient tools were also recovered. There were grindstones, milling stones, cutting blades, hide scrapers, engraving burins, and mortars and pestles. The level of the Nile 12,000 years ago was higher than it is now. Each year during the summer, the Nile flooded, depositing rich silt into the Wadi Kubbaniya region. As the waters receded in late August and September, catfish were left stranded in ponds that were formed by the depressions. Since ash and charcoal were also uncovered, it seems that the ancients smoked the fish. As the fish stocks were depleted the people took the opportunity to plant crops on the silt. After the planting, it seems that hunter gathering was the main activity, judging from the recovered bones. They hunted wild cattle, hartebeest and sometimes, hippos. When December or January arrived, this was the time for the harvest. The cereals were ground to make flour. After the harvest, gazelles became the main source of subsistence. Also hunted, were geese, ducks and wild game. By the time of summer, the Nile would flood again. The annual cycle was thus repeated.

Bayard Webster, in an article originally for the *New York Times*, explained Professor Nelson's view on the significance of these two important archaeological discoveries--agriculture and animal husbandry:

> Such findings suggest that many of the elements necessary for the development of civilization--agriculture and animal husbandry and their accompanying technologies--may have originated in surrounding areas and were exported to the Middle East through trade and cultural diffusion of information and ideas.

Mummification

The next major development in culture concerns a mummy found in the Acacus Mountains of south western Libya. Forty years ago a mummified infant was found under the Uan Muhuggiag rock shelter. The infant was buried in the fetal position and was mummified using a very sophisticated technique that must have taken hundreds of years to evolve. The technique predates the earliest mummies known in Ancient Egypt by at least 1,000 years. Carbon dating is controversial but the mummy may date from 7438 (±220) BC at the earliest, to 3500 BC at the latest.

Dr Savino di Lernia of the University of Rome took an interest in the mummy and also the culture that produced it. He believes that a widespread culture existed across a large part of Africa that encompassed the regions now designated as Mali, Niger, Chad, Sudan, Algeria, Libya and Egypt before this vast area became a desert. The rock art, for example, depicts elephants, giraffes, lions, crocodiles and hippopotami--many of these animals can only survive in savannah regions. Some of the earliest pottery associated with this culture dates back to around 7000 BC. In this widespread culture, cattle had a religious and ritualistic significance. There were circular temples built where cattle were sacrificed. Moreover, cattle appear in up to 50% of the rock art. There were also religious rituals involving humans wearing jackal headed masks depicted in the rock art. Also humans were typically buried in the fetal position. Initially Italian archaeologists believed this culture was unique to Libya but French archaeologists showed a similar culture existed in Niger 500 miles to the south.

Dr Joann Fletcher, the noteworthy English Egyptologist, believes that the mummification techniques of this culture informed later Egyptian mummification. She further believes that its cattle cult informed Egyptian religious ideas of a later period. Finally, she believes that its jackal mask rituals informed the Egyptian concept of Anubis, the god of embalming--depicted in Egyptian art as a jackal. Moreover, there is archaeological evidence that Uan Muhuggiag decorated pottery later appeared in the southern Nile Valley region. Dr di Lernia suggests that the Uan Muhuggiag people migrated to the Nile Valley when the region became a desert. Also, they became an integral part of the Ancient Egyptian culture. Dr Fletcher summarised the importance of these findings thus:

> I find it quite extraordinary that this central Saharan civilisation shows all the features we generally associate with later Egyptian pharaonic culture and mummification is a prime example. There are definite links between the two cultures.

Astronomy

In Nabta Playa, 100 km west of Abu Simbel, is an unpromising looking stone circle commonly called the Calendar Circle. The site is connected to the Saharan culture mentioned above. Astrophysicist Dr Thomas Brophy conducted a study of the site and published in 2002. He concluded that it was used between 6400 BC and 4900 BC for astronomical observance. Moreover, Wikipedia says these dates match 'the radio-carbon dating of campfires around the circle.' However, a study of the site conducted by a later team of scholars attempted to rubbish Dr Brophy's dates. Wikipedia reports:

> A 2007 article by a team of University of Colorado archaeoastronomers and archaeologists ... responded to the work of Brophy and Rosen, in particular their claims for an alignment with Sirius in 6088 [BC] and other alignments which they dated to 6270, saying that these dates were about 1500 years earlier than the estimated dates. The Sirius alignment in question was originally proposed by Wendorf and Malville, for one of the most prominent alignments of megaliths labelled the 'C-line', which they said aligned to the rising of Sirius circa 4820 BC. Brophy and Rosen showed in 2005 that megalith orientations and star positions reported by Wendorf and Malville were in error, noting that 'Given these corrected data, we see that Sirius actually aligned with the C line circa 6000 BC. We estimate that 6088 BC Sirius had a declination of -36.51 deg, for a rising azimuth exactly on the C-line average'.

How did Malville respond to being proved wrong? Wikipedia narrates:

> Malville acknowledged the corrections made by Brophy and Rosen, but concluded the C-line of megaliths 'may not represent an original set of aligned stele; we refrain from interpreting that alignment.'

African Proto Science and Technology

Figure 37. Nabta Playa Calendar Circle, reconstructed at the Aswan Nubia Museum (Photo: Raymbetz).

This is NOT a satisfactory response to having been proved wrong. I therefore conclude that the Brophy and Rosen dates have withstood the challenge of the 2007 team.

What did Dr Brophy find? He found that some of the stones were aligned to the summer solstice sunrise. Others were aligned in a north south position. Three of the six central megaliths were aligned to the three stars of Orion's Belt just before the summer solstice sunrise between the dates 6400 and 4900 BC. The three other megaliths may also have been astronomically aligned, but the details are controversial indeed and have led to many acrimonious intellectual debates.

There are other groups of stellar-aligned megaliths 500 metres away from the Calendar Circle. Dr Brophy calculated that some of the other megaliths were aligned to the heliacal rising of each of the three stars of Orion's Belt at the Vernal Equinox (Alnitak in 6450 BC, Alnilam in 6270 BC and Mintaka in 6080 BC). Other alignments were to the heliacal rising of three other stars of Orion at the Vernal Equinox (Betelgeuse in 5820 BC, Bellatrix at 5310 BC and Meissa in 5200 BC). Brophy also found alignments to Vega and also to Sirius.

Controversially, Brophy found that the alignments of the megaliths encode estimated distances of the selected stars from the earth! In his own words:

> Why would these designers of the site have made these distances kind of unattractive when they were so elegantly placing the alignments in the other aspects? And it occurred to me to look for other meaning for the distances to go along with the alignment meanings ... And finally, just for fun, I looked up the actual astrophysical distances to those stars--you can find it on Hipparcos satellite observatory website. They were very recently measured very accurately--and I was surprised to find the actual astrophysical distances are represented by the distances on the ground of the stones in each line for its star that it represents.

Dr Brophy reckoned that 1 metre on the ground represented a distance of 0.799 Light Years. For Bellatrix, he found that its stone marker was 318 metres away from what he calls the central radiating hub. Thus 318 x 0.799 = 254 Light Years. Strangely enough the Hipparcos site gave the actual distance from the earth to Bellatrix as 250 Light Years. To give a second example, for Betelgeuse, Brophy found its stone marker to be 537 metres away. Thus 537 x 0.799 = 428 Light Years. The Hipparcos site gave the distance from the earth to Betelgeuse as 430 Light Years. This all suggests a very sophisticated level of astronomy from the people of Nabta Playa.

Summing Up

It is important to show that Ancient Egyptian science and technology did not come out of nowhere. Prehistoric Africa possesses evidence of bladelet technology from between 182,000 and 74,000 years ago, conducted organised fishing 90,000 years ago, mining 43,000 years ago, a number system 37,000 years ago, animal husbandry 15,000 years ago, agriculture 12,000 years ago, mummification 9000 years ago, and astronomy 8000 years ago.

We have seen that scholars have speculated that harpoon points, number systems, animal husbandry, agriculture, astronomy, and mummification, have diffused from Inner Africa to Egypt. Others have speculated that people have diffused from Inner Africa to Egypt.

Much more remains to be discovered about African proto science and technology. We have only scratched the surface. John Weatherwax wrote a paper many years ago where he speculated what tool technologies Africa must have contributed to proto science and technology. I give him the final word:

> Those early Africans made hooks to catch fish, spears to hunt with, stone knives to cut with, the bola, with which to catch birds and animals, the blow-gun, the hammer, the stone axe, canoes and paddles, bags and buckets, poles for

carrying things, bows and arrows ... The bola, stone knives, paddles, spears, harpoons, bows and arrows, blow-guns, the hammer and the axe--all of them invented first by Africans--were the start of man's use of power ... Africans gave mankind the first machine. It was the fire stick. With it, man could have fire any time. With it, a camp fire could be set up almost any place. With it, the early Africans could roast food ... Knives and hammers and axes were the first tools. It is making of tools that sets man apart from and in a sense above all living creatures. Africans started mankind along the toolmaking path. Of course those early Africans were the first to discover how to make a thatched hut ... They discovered coarse basket-making and weaving and how to make a watertight pot of clay hardened in a fire. In cold weather, they found that the skins of beasts they had killed would keep them warm. They even made skin wraps for their feet. It was from these first efforts that (much later) clothing and shoes developed ... They domesticated the dog. They used digging sticks to get at roots that could be eaten. They discovered grain as a food, and how to store and prepare it. They learned about the fermentation of certain foods and liquids left in containers ... African hunters many times cut up game. There still exist, from the Old Stone Age, drawings of animal bones, hearts and other organs. Those early drawings are a part of man's early beginnings in the field of Anatomy.

BIBLIOGRAPHY

Preface

Bryan Hill, *Adam's Calendar: Oldest Megalithic Site in the World?* 2 June 2015, see http://www.ancient-origins.net/ancient-places-africa/adam-s-calendar-oldest-megalithic-site-world-003160

Introduction

Ivan Van Sertima, *Forward,* in *Blacks in Science: Ancient and Modern,* ed Ivan Van Sertima, US, Transaction Publishers, 1983, p.5

Ivan Van Sertima, *Teacher's Guide,* in *Blacks in Science: Ancient and Modern,* ed Ivan Van Sertima, US, Transaction Publishers, 1983, p.293

Tool Making

Bruce Boyer, *African finds revise cultural roots,* in *Science News Online: Editors' Picks,* 29 April 1995, see http://www.sciencenews.org/sn_edpik/aa_2.htm

Charles S. Finch, *The Star of Deep Beginnings,* US, Khenti, 1998, pp.2-7

Fari Supiya, *Appendix: Where from Here?* in *When We Ruled: Second Edition,* by Robin Walker, UK, Reklaw Education, 2013, pp.751-752

Mining

Yosef A. A. ben Jochannan, *Africa! Mother of Western Civilization,* US, Black Classic Press, 1971, p.56

Charles S. Finch, *The Star of Deep Beginnings,* US, Khenti, 1998, pp.25-27

Proto Mathematics

CNN, *The Ishango Bone,* see internet at https://www.youtube.com/watch?v=VX90lN8VSME

Charles S. Finch, *The Star of Deep Beginnings,* US, Khenti, 1998, pp.3, 4, 55-57

Robin Walker and John Matthews, *African Mathematics: History, Textbook and Classroom Lessons,* UK, Reklaw Education, 2014, pp.9-10

Claudia Zaslavsky, *Africa Counts,* US, Lawrence Hill & Co., 1973, pp.17-18

Animal Husbandry and Agriculture

Bayard Webster, *African Cattle Bones Stir Scientific Debate,* in *Blacks in Science: Ancient and Modern,* ed Ivan Van Sertima, US, Transaction Publishers, 1983, pp.65-66

Fred Wendorf, Romauld Schild, and Angela E. Close, *An Ancient Harvest on the Nile,* in *Blacks in Science: Ancient and Modern,* ed Ivan Van Sertima, US, Transaction Publishers, 1983, p.58

Mummification

Michael J. Carter, *The Infant Mummy of Uan Muhuggiag,* in *Egypt: Child of Africa,* ed Ivan Van Sertima, US, Transaction Publishers, 1994, pp.278-279

Gillian Mosely (producer), *The Black Mummy Mystery,* (television programme), UK, Fulcrum TV, 2003

Astronomy

Thomas Brophy is in John Anthony West, *Magical Egypt,* (television programme), US, 2001,
see https://www.youtube.com/watch?v=T42nRhpOHBg

Wikipedia, *Nabta Playa,* see https://en.wikipedia.org/wiki/Nabta_Playa

Summing Up

John Weatherwax, *The African Contribution,* quoted in John G. Jackson, *Introduction to African Civilizations,* US, Citadel Press, 1970, pp.22-24

Also available in this series

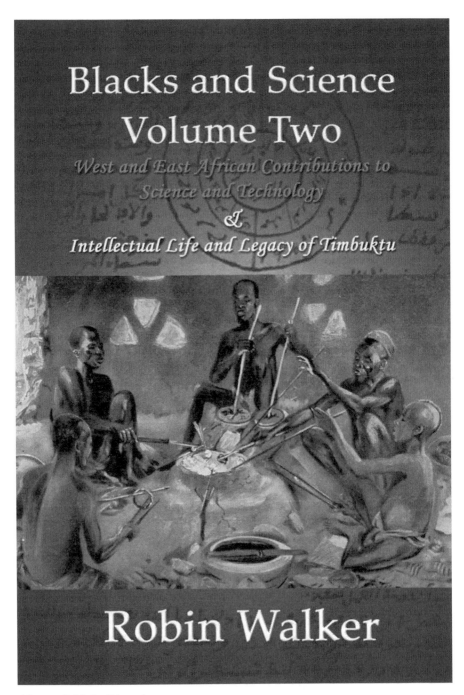

PART FOUR

EXCERPT FROM *AN INTRODUCTION TO THE HISTORY OF SCIENCE*, 1917

Excerpt from *An Introduction to the History of Science*

THE OPINIONS OF PROFESSOR WALTER LIBBY

Introduction

Professor Walter Libby wrote an excellent work on the origin and evolution of science in 1917 entitled *An Introduction to the History of Science* (US, The Riverside Press, pp.1-15). His opening chapter concerns the scientific and technological contributions of the Ancient Egyptians and the Ancient peoples of Iraq and Syria. I do not agree with every single word in the chapter, but it is always good to read and profit from other opinions. Moreover, the main points of difference between my views and his are relatively trivial. I still emphasize that this is a great piece of scholarship and he has mentioned many Egyptian discoveries that have not been addressed elsewhere in this book.

Excerpt: *Science and practical needs Egypt and Babylonia*

If you consult encyclopedias and special works in reference to the early history of any one of the sciences,--astronomy, geology, geometry, physiology, logic, or political science, for example,--you will find strongly emphasized the part played by the Greeks in the development of organized knowledge. Great, indeed, as we shall see in the next chapter, are the contributions to the growth of science of this highly rational and speculative people. It must be conceded, also, that the influence on Western science of civilizations earlier than theirs has come to us, to a considerable extent at least, through the channels of Greek literature.

Nevertheless, if you seek the very origins of the sciences, you will inevitably be drawn to the banks of the Nile, and to the valleys of the Tigris and the Euphrates. Here, in Egypt, in Assyria and Babylonia, dwelt from very remote times nations whose genius was practical and religious rather than intellectual and theoretical, and whose mental life, therefore, was more akin to our own than was the highly evolved culture of the Greeks. Though more remote in time, the wisdom and practical knowledge of Thebes and Memphis, Nineveh and Babylon, are more readily comprehended by our minds than the difficult speculations of Athenian philosophy.

Much that we have inherited from the earliest civilizations is so familiar, so homely, that we simply accept it, much as we may light, or air, or water, without analysis, without inquiry as to its origin, and without full recognition of how indispensable it is. Why are there seven days in the week, and not eight? Why are there sixty minutes in the hour, and why are there not sixty hours in the day? These artificial divisions of time are accepted so unquestioningly that to ask a reason for them may, to an indolent mind, seem almost absurd. This acceptance of a week of seven days and of an hour of sixty minutes (almost as if they were natural divisions of time like day and night) is owing to a tradition that is Babylonian in its origin. From the Old Testament (which is one of the greatest factors in preserving the continuity of human culture, and the only ancient book which speaks with authority concerning Babylonian history) we learn that Abraham, the progenitor of the Hebrews, migrated to the west from southern Babylonia about twenty-three hundred years before Christ. Even in that remote age, however, the Babylonians had established those divisions of time which are familiar to us. The seven days of the week were closely associated in men's thinking with the heavenly bodies. In our modern languages they are named after the sun, the moon, Mars, Mercury, Jupiter, Venus, and Saturn, which from the remotest times were personified and worshiped. Thus we see that the usage of making seven days a unit of time depends on the religious belief and astronomical science of a very remote civilization. The usage is so completely established that by the majority it is simply taken for granted.

Another piece of commonplace knowledge--the cardinal points of the compass--may be accepted, likewise, without inquiry or without recognition of its importance. Unless thrown on your own resources in an unsettled country or on unknown waters, you may long fail to realize how indispensable to the practical conduct of life is the knowledge of east and west and north and south. In this matter, again, the records of ancient civilizations show the pains that were taken to fix these essentials of science. Modern excavations have demonstrated that the sides or the corners of the temples and palaces of Assyria and Babylonia were directed to the four cardinal points of the compass. In Egypt the pyramids, erected before 3000 B.C., were laid out with such strict regard to direction that the conjecture has been put forward that their main purpose was to establish, in a land of shifting sands, east and west and north and south. That conjecture seems extravagant; but the fact that the Phœnicians studied astronomy merely because of its practical value in navigation, the early invention of

Excerpt from *An Introduction to the History of Science*

the compass in China, the influence on discovery of the later improvements of the compass, make us realize the importance of the alleged purpose of the pyramids. Without fixed points, without something to go by, men, before they had acquired the elements of astronomy, were altogether at sea. As they advanced in knowledge they looked to the stars for guidance, especially to the pole star and the imperishable star-group of the northern heavens. The Egyptians even developed an apparatus for telling the time by reference to the stars--a star-clock similar in its purpose to the sundial. By the Egyptians, also, was carefully observed the season of the year at which certain stars and constellations were visible at dawn. This was of special importance in the case of Sirius, for its heliacal rising, that is, the period when it rose in conjunction with the sun, marked the coming of the Nile flood (so important in the lives of the inhabitants) and the beginning of a new year. Not unnaturally Sirius was an object of worship. One temple is said to have been so constructed as to face that part of the eastern horizon at which this star arose at the critical season of inundation. Of another temple we are told that only at sunset at the time of the summer solstice did the sun throw its rays throughout the edifice. The fact that astronomy in Egypt as in Babylonia, where the temples were observatories, was closely associated with religion confirms the view that this science was first cultivated because of its bearing on the practical needs of the people. The priests were the preservers of such wisdom as had been accumulated in the course of man's immemorial struggle with the forces of nature.

It is well known that geometry had its origin in the valley of the Nile, that it arose to meet a practical need, and that it was in the first place, as its name implies, a measurement of the earth--a crude surveying, employed in the restoration of boundaries obliterated by the annual inundations of the river. Egyptian geometry cared little for theory. It addressed itself to actual problems, such as determining the area of a square or triangular field from the length of the sides. To find the area of a circular field, or floor, or vessel, from the length of the diameter was rather beyond the science of 2000 B.C. This was, however, a practical problem which had to be solved, even if the solution were not perfect. The practice was to square the diameter reduced by one ninth.

In all the Egyptian mathematics of which we have record there is to be observed a similar practical bent. In the construction of a temple or a pyramid not merely was it necessary to have regard to the points of the compass, but care must be taken to have the sides at right angles. This required the intervention of specialists, expert 'rope-fasteners,' who laid off a triangle by means of a rope divided into three parts, of three, four, and five units. The Babylonians followed much the same practice in fixing a right angle. In addition they learned how to bisect and trisect the angle. Hence we see in their designs and ornaments the division of the circle into twelve parts, a division which does not appear in Egyptian ornamentation till after the incursion of Babylonian influence.

There is no need, however, to multiply examples; the tendency of all Egyptian mathematics was, as already stated, concerned with the practical solution of concrete problems--mensuration, the cubical contents of barns and granaries, the distribution of bread, the amounts of food required by men and animals in given numbers and for given periods of time, the proportions and the angle of elevation (about 52°) of a pyramid, etc. Moreover, they worked simple equations involving one unknown, and had a hieroglyph for a million (the drawing of a man overcome with wonder), and another for ten million.

The Rhind mathematical papyrus in the British Museum is the main source of our present knowledge of early Egyptian arithmetic, geometry, and of what might be called their trigonometry and algebra. It describes itself as 'Instructions for arriving at the knowledge of all things, and of things obscure, and of all mysteries.' It was copied by a priest about 1600 B.C.--the classical period of Egyptian culture--from a document seven hundred years older.

Medicine, which is almost certain to develop in the early history of a people in response to their urgent needs, has been justly called the foster-mother of many sciences. In the records of Egyptian medical practice can be traced the origin of chemistry, anatomy, physiology, and botany. Our most definite information concerning Egyptian medicine belongs to the same general period as the mathematical document to which we have just referred. It is true something is known of remoter times. The first physician of whom history has preserved the name, I-em-hetep (He-who-cometh-in-peace), lived about 4500 B.C. Recent researches have also brought to light, near Memphis, pictures, not later than 2500 B.C., of surgical operations. They were found sculptured on the doorposts at the entrance to the tomb of a high official of one of the Pharaohs. The patients, as shown in the accompanying illustration, are suffering pain, and, according to the inscription, one cries out, 'Do this [and] let me go,' and the other, 'Don't hurt me so!' Our most satisfactory data in reference to Egyptian medicine are derived, however, from the Ebers papyrus. This document displays some little knowledge of the pulse in different parts of the body, of a relation between the heart and the other organs, and of the passage of the breath to the lungs (and heart). It contains a list of diseases. In the main it is a collection of prescriptions for the eyes, ears, stomach, to reduce tumors, effect purgation, etc. There is no evidence of a tendency to homeopathy, but mental healing seems to have been called into play by the use of numerous spells and incantations. Each prescription, as in medical practice to-day, contains as a rule several ingredients. Among the seven hundred recognized remedies are to be noted poppy, castor-oil, gentian, colchicum, squills, and many other familiar medicinal plants, as well as bicarbonate of soda, antimony, and salts of lead and copper. The fat of the lion, hippopotamus, crocodile, goose, serpent, and wild goat, in equal parts, served as a prescription for baldness. In the interests of his art the medical practitioner ransacked the resources of organic and inorganic nature. The Ebers papyrus shows that the Egyptians knew of the development of the beetle from the egg, of the blow-fly from the larva, and of the frog from the tadpole. Moreover, for precision in the use of medicaments weights of very small denominations were employed.

The Egyptian embalmers relied on the preservative properties of common salt, wine, aromatics, myrrh, cassia, etc. By the use of linen smeared with

Figure 38. Libby gave the caption: **Earliest picture known of a surgical operation.** Egypt, 2500 B.C.

gum they excluded all putrefactive agencies. They understood the virtue of extreme dryness in the exercise of their antiseptic art. Some knowledge of anatomy was involved in the removal of the viscera, and much more in a particular method they followed in removing the brain.

In their various industries the Egyptians made use of gold, silver, bronze (which on analysis is found to consist of copper, tin, and a trace of lead, etc.), metallic iron and copper and their oxides, manganese, cobalt, alum, cinnabar, indigo, madder, brass, white lead, lampblack. There is clear evidence that they smelted iron ore as early as 3400 B.C. maintaining a blast by means of leather tread-bellows. They also contrived to temper the metal, and to make helmets, swords, lance-points, ploughs, tools, and other implements of iron. Besides metallurgy they practiced the arts of weaving, dyeing, distillation. They produced soap (from soda and oil), transparent and colored glass, enamel, and ceramics. They were skilled in the preparation of leather. They showed aptitude for painting, and for the other fine arts. They were expert builders, and possessed the engineering skill to erect obelisks weighing hundreds of tons. They cultivated numerous vegetables, grains, fruits, and flowers. They had many domestic animals. In seeking the satisfaction of their practical needs they laid the foundation of geometry, botany, chemistry (named, as some think, from the Egyptian Khem, the god of medicinal herbs), and other sciences. But their practical achievements far transcended their theoretical formulations. To all time they will be known as an artistic, noble, and religious people, who cherished their dead and would not allow that the good and beautiful and great should altogether pass away.

Excavations in Assyria and Babylonia, especially since 1843, have brought to our knowledge an ancient culture stretching back four or five thousand years before the beginning of the Christian era. The records of Assyria and Babylonia, like those of Egypt, are fragmentary and still in need of interpretation. Here again, however, it is the fundamental, the indispensable, the practical forms of knowledge that stand revealed rather than the theoretical, speculative, and purely intellectual.

By the Babylonian priests the heavens were made the object of expert observation as early as 3800 B.C. The length of the year, the length of the month, the coming of the seasons, the course of the sun in the heavens, the movements of the planets, the recurrence of eclipses, comets, and meteors, were studied with particular care. One motive was the need of a measurement of time, the same motive as underlies the common interest in the calendar and almanac. It was found that the year contained more than 365 days, the month (synodic) more than 29 days, 12 hours, and 44 minutes. The sun's apparent diameter was contained 720 times in the ecliptic, that is, in the apparent path of the sun through the heavens. Like the Egyptians, the Babylonians took special note of the stars and star-groups that were to be seen at dawn at different times of the year. These constellations, lying in the imaginary belt encircling the heavens on either side of the ecliptic, bore names corresponding to those we have adopted for the signs of the zodiac,--Balance, Ram, Bull, Twins, Scorpion, Archer, etc. The Babylonian astronomers also observed that the successive vernal (or autumnal) equinoxes follow each other at intervals of a few seconds less than a year.

A second motive that influenced the Babylonian priests in studying the movements of the heavenly bodies was the hope of foretelling events. The planets, seen to shift their positions with reference to the other heavenly bodies, were called messengers, or angels. The appearance of Mars, perhaps on account of its reddish color, was associated in their imaginations with war. Comets, meteors, and eclipses were considered as omens portending pestilence, national disaster, or the fate of kings. The fortunes of individuals could be predicted from a knowledge of the aspect of the heavens at the hour of their birth. This interest in astrology, or divination by means of the stars, no doubt stimulated the priests to make careful observations and to preserve religiously the record of astronomical phenomena. It was even established that there is a cycle in which eclipses, solar and lunar, repeat themselves, a period (saros) somewhat more than eighteen years and eleven months. Moreover, from the Babylonians we derive some of our most sublime religious and scientific conceptions. They held that strict law governs the apparently erratic movements of the heavenly bodies. Their creation myth proclaims: 'Merodach next arranged the stars in order, along with the sun and moon, and gave them laws which they were never to transgress.'

The mathematical knowledge of the Babylonians is related on the one hand to their astronomy and on the other to their commercial pursuits. They possessed highly developed systems of measuring, weighing, and counting-processes, which, as we shall see in the sequel, are essential to scientific thought. About 2300 B.C. they had multiplication tables running from 1 to 1350, which were probably used in connection with astronomical calculations. Unlike the Egyptians they had no symbol for a million, though the 'ten thousand times ten thousand' of the Bible (Daniel VII: 10) may indicate that the conception of even larger numbers was not altogether foreign to them. They counted in sixties as well as in tens. Their hours and minutes had each sixty subdivisions. They divided the circle into six parts and into six-times-sixty subdivisions. Tables of squares and cubes discovered in southern Babylonia were interpreted correctly only on a sexagesimal basis, the statement that 1 plus 4 is the square of 8 implying that the first unit is 60. As we have already seen, considerable knowledge of geometry is apparent in Babylonian designs and constructions.

According to a Greek historian of the fifth century B.C., there were no physicians at Babylon, while a later Greek historian (of the first century B.C.) speaks of a Babylonian university which had attained celebrity, and which is now believed to have been a school of medicine. Modern research has made known letters by a physician addressed to an Assyrian king in the seventh century B.C. referring to the king's chief physician, giving directions for the treatment of a bleeding from the nose from which a friend of the prince was suffering, and reporting the probable recovery of a poor fellow whose eyes were diseased. Other letters from the same general period mention the presence of physicians at court. We have even recovered the name (Ilu-bani) of a physician who lived in southern Babylonia about 2700 B.C. The most interesting information, however, in reference to Babylonian medicine dates from the time of Hammurabi, a contemporary of the patriarch Abraham. It appears from the code drawn up in the reign of that monarch that the Babylonian surgeons operated in case of cataract; that they were entitled to twenty silver shekels (half the sum for which Joseph was sold into slavery, and equivalent to seven or eight dollars) for a successful operation; and that in case the patient lost his life or his sight as the result of an unsuccessful operation, the surgeon was condemned to have his hands amputated.

The Babylonian records of medicine like those of astronomy reveal the prevalence of many superstitious beliefs. The spirits of evil bring maladies upon us; the gods heal the diseases that afflict us. The Babylonian books of medicine contained strange interminglings of prescription and incantation. The priests studied the livers of sacrificial animals in order to divine the thoughts of the gods--a practice which stimulated the study of anatomy. The maintenance of state menageries no doubt had a similar influence on the study of the natural history of animals.

The Babylonians were a nation of agriculturists and merchants. Sargon of Akkad, who founded the first Semitic empire in Asia (3800 B.C.), was brought up by an irrigator, and was himself a gardener. Belshazzar, the son

Excerpt from *An Introduction to the History of Science*

of the last Babylonian king, dealt in wool on a considerable scale. Excavation in the land watered by the Tigris and Euphrates tells the tale of the money-lenders, importers, dyers, fullers, tanners, saddlers, smiths, carpenters, shoemakers, stonecutters, ivory-cutters, brickmakers, porcelain-makers, potters, vintners, sailors, butchers, engineers, architects, painters, sculptors, musicians, dealers in rugs, clothing and fabrics, who contributed to the culture of this great historic people. It is not surprising that science should find its matrix in so rich a civilization.

The lever and the pulley, lathes, picks, saws, hammers, bronze operating-lances, sundials, water clocks, the gnomon (a vertical pillar for determining the sun's altitude) were in use. Gem-cutting was highly developed as early as 3800 B.C. The Babylonians made use of copper hardened with antimony and tin, lead, incised shells, glass, alabaster, lapis-lazuli, silver, and gold. Iron was not employed before the period of contact with Egyptian civilization. Their buildings were furnished with systems of drains and flushes that seem to us altogether modern. Our museums are enriched by specimens of their handicraft--realistic statuary in dolerite of 2700 B.C.; rock crystal worked to the form of a plano-convex lens, 3800 B.C.; a beautiful silver vase of the period 3950 B.C.; and the head of a goat in copper about 4000 B.C.

Excavation has not disclosed nor scholarship interpreted the full record of this ancient people in the valley of the Tigris and the Euphrates, not far from the Gulf of Persia, superior in religious inspiration, not inferior in practical achievements to the Egyptians. Both these great nations of antiquity, however, failed to carry the sciences that arose in connection with their arts to a high degree of generalization. That was reserved for another people of ancient times, namely, the Greeks.

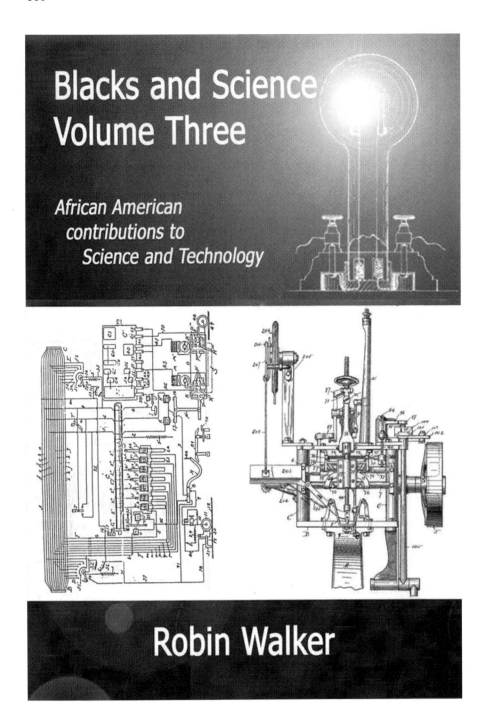

Also available in this series

PART FIVE

THE AUTHOR

The Author

ROBIN WALKER

Biography

Robin Walker 'The Black History Man' was born in London but has also lived in Jamaica. He attended the London School of Economics and Political Science where he read Economics.

In 1991 and 1992, he studied African World Studies with the brilliant Dr Femi Biko and later with Mr Kenny Bakie. Between 1993 and 1994, he trained as a secondary school teacher at Edge Hill College (linked to the University of Lancaster).

Since 1992 and up to the present period, Robin Walker has lectured in adult education, taught university short courses, and chaired conferences in African World Studies, Egyptology and Black History. The venues have been in Toxteth (Liverpool), Manchester, Leeds, Bradford, Huddersfield, Birmingham, Cambridge, Buckinghamshire and London.

Since 1994 he has taught Economics, Business & Finance, Mathematics, Information Communications Technology, PSHE/Citizenship and also History at various schools in London and Essex.

In 1999 he wrote *Classical Splendour: Roots of Black History* published in the UK by Bogle L'Ouverture Publications. In the same year, he co-authored (with Siaf Millar) *The West African Empire of Songhai*, a textbook used by many schools across the country.

In 2000 he co-authored (again with Siaf Millar) *Sword, Seal and Koran*, another book on the Songhai Empire of West Africa.

In 2006 he wrote the seminal *When We Ruled*. This is still the most advanced synthesis on Ancient and Mediaeval African history ever written by a single author. It was a massive expansion of his earlier book *Classical Splendour: Roots of Black History* and established his reputation as the leading Black History educational service provider.

In 2008 he wrote *Before The Slave Trade*, a highly pictorial companion volume to *When We Ruled*.

Between 2011 and 2014 he wrote a series of e-books for download sold through Amazon Kindle. These e-books covered history, business, religion, music, and science.

In 2013 he co-authored (with Siaf Millar and Saran Keita) *Everyday Life*

In An Early West African Empire. It was a massive expansion on the earlier book *Sword, Seal & Koran*. He updated *When We Ruled* by incorporating nearly all of the images from *Before The Slave Trade*. He wrote a trilogy of books entitled *Blacks and Science Volumes One, Two* and *Three*.

In 2014 he wrote *The Rise and Fall of Black Wall $treet and the Seven Key Empowerment Principles, Blacks and Religion Volume One* and *If you want to learn Early African History START HERE*. He also co-authored *African Mathematics: History, Textbook and Classroom Lessons* (with John Matthews).

In 2015 he wrote *19 Lessons in Black History* and *The Black Musical Tradition and Early Black Literature*. He also wrote *Blacks and Religion Volume Two*.

Speaking Engagements

Looking for a speaker for your next event?

The author Robin Walker 'The Black History Man' is dynamic and engaging, both as a speaker and a workshop leader. He brings Black or African history alive, making it relevant for the present generation. You will love his perfect blend of accessibility, engagement, and academic rigour where learning becomes fun.

Walker is available to give speaking engagements to a variety of audiences. Many will appreciate his lectures *Ancient Egyptian Contributions to Science and Technology* and *Mysterious Sciences of the Great Pyramid*.

To book Robin Walker for your next event, send an email to historicalwalker@yahoo.com

Also available

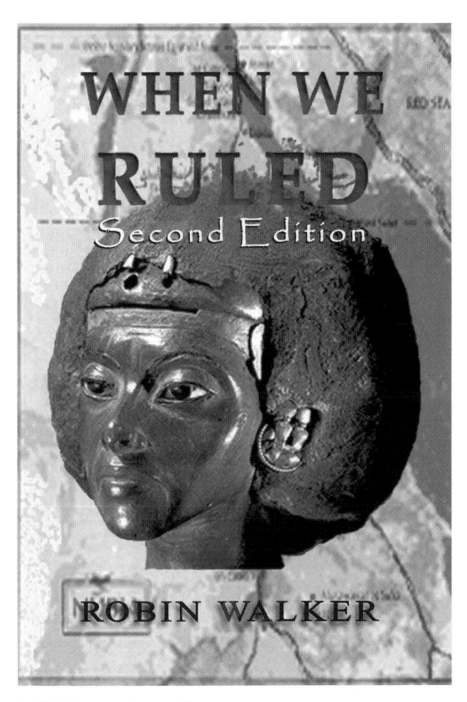

Available from www.whenweruled.com

INDEX

Abu Simbel Temple 45
Adam's Calendar 85-86
Adams, Hunter Havelin 5, 9, 46, 47, 48
Adams, Walter Marsham 57-58, 66-67
adhesives 9, 24
Agarthachides 70-71
aeronautics 47-48
agriculture 9
alcohol 9
algebra 11, 104
al-Jahith 5
Al-Khalili, Jim 5
Allen, Richard 20
alloys 9, 48
animal husbandry 90-91
antibiotics 26, 28
antiseptics 106
architecture 38-45, 57-65
Aristotle 11
astronomy 15-21, 71, 88-89, 92-94, 102-103
atomos 7, 9

Bauval, Robert 64-66, 68
ben Jochannan, Yosef 85, 86
Berlin Mathematical Papyrus 11, 13
BIS Publications 1
Bovis, M. 76
Breasted, James Henry 59
Brooks, Alison 87
Brophy, Thomas 92-94
Browder, Anthony 64
Budge, E. A. W. 17
building materials 9, 38

calendar 15-17, 75, 88-89
cartography 35-37
Chandler, Wayne 62-63
Cheops Pyramid Razorblade Sharpeners 76
chlorophyll 20-21

Churchward, Albert 17
circumpolar constellations 19-20
clocks 7, 8, 15, 103
contraception 24, 28
cosmetics 9
cubit 7, 9, 14, 69-70, 74
cylinder 11, 12, 13

Dart, Raymond 87-88
Darwin, Charles 5
decimal system 11, 89
De Heinzelin, Jean 89-90
Deir-el-Bahri Temple 29, 45
dentistry 24, 25
diagnostic method 24, 25
diatonic scale 46
diffusionism 35
Diop, Cheikh Anta 5, 12, 27-28
distance 7, 48
Djibrine, Abdullah 30
Drbal, Karel 76
Dunn, Christopher 76-79
dyes 9

Ebers Papyrus 24-25, 105
eclipse, lunar 18-19
Edwin Smith Surgical Papyrus 22-23, 25
electroplating 46
Elleh, Nnamdi 6, 45
evolution, theory of 5

fibres 9
Finch, Charles 5, 22-24, 25, 29, 37, 40, 48, 85, 86, 89-90
Fletcher, Joann 91-92
fractions 11
Funerary Complex at Saqqara 38-40

geometry 11-14, 103-104
glazed ware 9

glider 47-48
Golden Section 14, 71-74
Goodman, Charles 20
Great Year 19-20
gums 9

Haber, Louis 5
Hancock, Graham 64-66, 68
Hapgood, Charles 32, 35-37
harmonics 46
heliocentric theory 18
heqat 9
Herodotus 42, 55, 62, 72-74
Heyerdahl, Thor 29-31
Hill, Bryan 85-86
Hippocrates 25, 27-28
Holmes, Keith 1, 9-10
Homer 22
hour 8, 15, 16, 19, 25

Imhotep (also I-em-hetep) 27-28, 38, 104
ink 9
irrational numbers 14, 65-66, 74-75
Ishango Bone 89

Jairazbhoy, Rafique Ali 32, 34, 35, 37

Kahun, city of 40-42
Kahun Papyrus 11, 13
Karnak Temple 42-45
Kelly, Patricia 89
Khufu, Pharaoh 17, 19, 29, 55, 60-61, 76

Labyrinth, The 42
Lebombo Bone 88-89
Lemesurier, Peter 55, 69-70, 79
length 7, 9, 48, 69-70, 74
Libby, Walter 2, 99-109
light, speed of 21
Lockyer, Norman 20, 21
Lumpkin, Beatrice 14, 33, 75

MacNaughton, Duncan 15, 16, 19, 59
Manetho 22, 59-60
Mariette, Auguste 46
Maspero, Gaston 63
mass 7
materia medica 26, 105-106

mathematics 11-14, 103-104
mathematics, proto 88-89
medicine 22-28, 48, 104-106
Melgar, José M. 31-32
merkhet 15
Mesopotamian Science 106-109
Messiha, Khalil 47
metals and metallurgy 9, 46, 48, 106
Meyer, Eduard 59-60
minerals 9
mining 87-88
Mokhtar, Gamal 47
monad 9
moon, the 15, 18-19, 88-89
Moscow Mathematical Papyrus 11, 13
mummification 24, 105-106
music 46

Nabta Playa 92-94
navigation 29-37
Newton, Isaac 9, 18, 69
number system 7, 11, 88-89, 104

obelisks 29, 43-45
Obenga, Théophile 6, 12, 20-21, 23, 24, 25, 46
oils 9
Olmec Civilisation 31-37

paints 9-10
Pappademos, John 29
Patten-Van Sertima, Jacqueline 33-35
Petrie, W. M. F. 59-60, 63-64, 76-78
pharmacopeia 26
phi (or φ) 14, 71-74
photosynthesis 21
pi (or π) 12, 13, 14, 65, 66
pigments 9-10
Piri Re'is 32, 35-37
planets 15, 18
Plutarch 14
Pochan, André 59-60, 75
pottery 10
precession of the equinoxes 19-20, 21
pregnancy diagnosis 24, 28
Pyramids 13, 32, 33, 38, 40
Pyramid, Great 14, 40, 55-82
Pythagorean Theorem 13-14, 103-104

Index

qedet 9

remen 14, 75
resins 9
Rhind Mathematical Papyrus 11-12, 104
ruler 7

sarcophagus, 76-79
scales 7, 8
series, mathematical 12-13
ships 29-37
Sirius 20, 92, 93, 103
Sothiac Cycle 16-17
sphere 13
spices 10, 24
Stecchini, Livio Catullo 9, 70
stones, precious 10
Strabo 17
sun, the 15, 16, 18-21, 71, 75, 79, 85
sundial 15
Supiya, Fari 85, 86, 87
surgery 22-25, 104-106

Taylor, John 65
textiles 10
time 7, 9, 15, 48
Tompkins, Peter 56, 69, 74
tool making 48, 76-79, 87, 88, 94-95
town planning 40-42
trapezium 12
trigonometry 12, 104
truncated pyramid 13

Uan Muhuggiag 91-92

Van Sertima, Ivan 5, 32-33, 37, 85, 86, 87
volume 7, 9, 12, 48
Von Wuthenau, Alexander 32, 33
Vyse, Howard 60

Walker, Robin 113-114
Wallace, Alfred Russell 40, 64-65, 66
Weatherwax, John 94-95
Webster, Bayard 91
weight 7, 8, 9, 48
Wendorf, Fred 90, 92
Wiercinski, Andrej 32, 33, 37
Winters, Clyde-Ahmad 85, 86

wood 10

zodiac 17-20, 107

Available from www.everydaylifeinanearlywestafricanempire.com

Made in the USA
Middletown, DE
02 September 2024

60178325R00071